THE KEY

STUDENT STUDY GUIDE

Social Studies 9

THE KEY

THE KEY series of student study guides is specifically designed to assist students in preparing for unit tests, provincial achievement tests, and diploma examinations. Each ***KEY*** includes questions, answers, detailed solutions, and practice tests. The complete solutions show problem-solving methods, explain key concepts, and highlight potential errors.

TABLE OF CORRELATIONS

Castle Rock Research has designed ***THE KEY*** by correlating every question and its solution to Alberta Education's curriculum outcomes. Each unit of review begins with a Table of Correlations that lists the General and Specific Outcomes from the Alberta curriculum along with Related Questions that correspond to the outcomes. Usually the emphasis placed on outcomes, concepts, and skills within each unit varies. Students and teachers can quickly identify the relevant importance of each outcome and concept in the unit as determined by the number of related questions provided in ***THE KEY***.

For grades 3, 6, 9, and 12, the weighting of each unit and concept is determined by analyzing the blueprint for the respective provincial achievement tests and diploma examinations. Based on this analysis, the Related Questions for outcomes and concepts are organized on a proportionate basis. For grades other than 3, 6, 9, and 12, the breakdown of each course is determined by consulting with experienced teachers and by reviewing curriculum guides and textbooks.

The Table of Correlations is a critical component of ***THE KEY***. For students, it offers a visual cue for effectively organizing study time. For teachers, the Table of Correlations indicates the instructional focus for each content strand, serves as a curriculum checklist, and focuses on the outcomes and concepts that are the most important in the unit and the particular course of study. Students become "test wise" by becoming familiar with exam and question formats used most often in provincial examinations.

Canadian Cataloguing in Publication Data

Rao, Gautam, 1961 –
THE KEY – Social Studies 9

1. Social Studies – Juvenile Literature. I. Title

Published by
Castle Rock Research Corp.
2340 Manulife Place
10180 – 101 Street
Edmonton, AB T5J 3S4

5 6 7 FP 07 06 05

Printed in Canada

Publisher:
Gautam Rao

Editors:
Mun Prasad
Shirley Wacowich

Contributors:
Richard Clayton
Rick Bookham
Andrew Gambier

Print Production:
Phil Beauchamp
Alesha Braitenbach
Nishi Chadha
Kevin Huenison
Lorraine James
James Kropfreiter
Julie May
David Moret
Suzanne Morin
Jackie Pacheco
Tara Pratt
Abhinav Rastogi
Diana Seguin
Jan Witwicky
Gary Yaremchuk
Richard Yeomans

Castle Rock Research Corp

Dedicated to the memory of Dr. V. S. Rao

THE KEY – SOCIAL STUDIES 9

THE KEY is a study guide specifically designed to complement classroom instruction and assist students in preparing for unit exams and their provincial achievement test. It is a compilation of questions and answers from previous Provincial Achievement Tests complete with detailed solutions for all questions. Questions have been grouped by concepts so that students can use the resource in their studies throughout the year. Working through these exercises should help students to reinforce the course material and identify those areas that may require more review. **Complete solutions for all questions are provided** to assist students in understanding the concept and the problem solving used to arrive at the correct answer. ***THE KEY*** is organized into the following sections.

I ***KEY Factors Contributing to School Success*** provides students with examples of study and review strategies. Topics include information on learning styles, study schedules, and developing review notes.

II ***Unit Review***, with *Challenger Questions*, includes questions related to *Economic Growth: USA; Economic Growth: Former USSR;* and *Economic Growth: Canada.* Each unit begins with a Table of Correlations in which the questions are classified according to the specific learner outcomes of the curriculum. In *Unit Review*, questions considered to be more difficult are labeled as *Challenger* questions. By emphasizing questions of a more challenging nature, it is hoped that students will become more familiar with the depth of knowledge required to achieve at the standard of excellence. ***THE KEY*** **provides detailed solutions for all questions.**

III ***KEY Strategies for Success on Exams*** explores topics such as common exam question formats and strategies for responding, directing words most commonly used, how to begin the exam, and managing test anxiety.

IV The ***Provincial Achievement Test Preparation*** section contains the provincial achievement tests that were administered in 2000 and 2001. The questions presented here are distinct from the questions in the previous sections. It is **recommended** that students work through these exams carefully as they are reflective of the exam format and level of difficulty that students are likely to encounter on their final exams. **Complete solutions are provided for all questions in this section.**

THE KEY *Study Guides* are available for Language Arts 9, Mathematics 9, Science 9, and Social Studies 9. A complete list of the ***THE KEY*** *Study Guides* available for Grades 3 to 12 is included at the back of this book.

For information about any of our resources or services, please call Castle Rock Research Corp. at 780.448.9619 or visit our web site at http://www.castlerockresearch.com.

At Castle Rock Research, we strive to produce a resource that is error-free. If you should find an error, please contact us so that future editions can be corrected.

CONTENTS

KEY FACTORS CONTRIBUTING TO SCHOOL SUCCESS

UNIT REVIEW

ANSWERS AND SOLUTIONS – UNIT REVIEW

KEY STRATEGIES FOR SUCCESS ON EXAMS

PROVINCIAL ACHIEVEMENT TEST PREPARATION

ANSWERS AND SOLUTIONS – PROVINCIAL ACHIEVEMENT TEST

APPENDICES

KEY FACTORS CONTRIBUTING TO SCHOOL SUCCESS

KEY FACTORS CONTRIBUTING TO SCHOOL SUCCESS

You want to do well in school. There are many factors that contribute to your success. While you may not have control over the number or types of assignments and tests that you need to complete, there are many factors that you can control to improve your academic success in any subject area. The following are examples of these factors.

- **REGULAR CLASS ATTENDANCE** – helps you to master the subject content, identify key concepts, take notes and receive important handouts, ask your teacher questions, clarify information, use school resources, and meet students with whom you can study
- **POSITIVE ATTITUDE AND PERSONAL DISCIPLINE** – helps you to come to classes on time, prepared to work and learn, complete all assignments to the best of your ability, and contribute to a positive learning environment
- **SELF-MOTIVATION AND PERSONAL DISCIPLINE** – helps you to set personal learning goals, take small steps continually moving toward achieving your goals, and to "stick it out when the going gets tough"
- **ACCESSING ASSISTANCE WHEN YOU NEED IT** – helps you to improve or clarify your understanding of the concept or new learning before moving on to the next phase
- **MANAGING YOUR TIME EFFICIENTLY** – helps you to reduce anxiety and focus your study and review efforts on the most important concepts
- **DEVELOPING 'TEST WISENESS'** – helps to increase your confidence in writing exams if you are familiar with the typical exam format, common errors to avoid, and know how the concepts in a subject area are usually tested
- **KNOWING YOUR PERSONAL LEARNING STYLE** – helps you to maximize your learning by using effective study techniques, developing meaningful study notes, and make the most efficient use of your study time

KNOW YOUR LEARNING STYLE

You have a unique learning style. Knowing your learning style – how you learn best – can help you to maximize your time in class and during your exam preparation. There are seven common learning styles. Read the following descriptions to see which one most closely describes your learning preferences.

- **LINGUISTIC LEARNER** (sometimes referred to as an auditory learner) – learns best by saying, hearing and seeing words; is good at memorizing things such as dates, places, names and facts
- **LOGICAL/MATHEMATICAL LEARNER** – learns best by categorizing, classifying and working with abstract relationships; is good at mathematics, problem solving and reasoning
- **SPATIAL LEARNER** (sometimes referred to as a visual learner) – learns best by visualizing, seeing, working with pictures; is good at puzzles, imaging things, and reading maps and charts
- **MUSICAL LEARNER** – learns best by hearing, rhythm, melody, and music; is good at remembering tones, rhythms and melodies, picking up sounds
- **BODILY/KINESTHETIC LEARNER** – learns best by touching, moving, and processing knowledge through bodily sensations; is good at physical activities
- **INTERPERSONAL LEARNER** – learns best by sharing, comparing, relating, cooperating; is good at organizing, communicating, leading, and understanding others
- **INTRAPERSONAL LEARNER** – learns best by working alone, individualized projects, and self-paced instruction

(Adapted from http://snow.utoronto.ca/Learn2/mod3/mistyles.html)

Your learning style may not fit "cleanly" into one specific category but may be a combination of two or more styles. Knowing your personal learning style allows you to organize your study notes in a manner that provides you with the most meaning. For example, if you are a spatial or visual learner, you may find mind mapping and webbing are effective ways to organize subject concepts, information, and study notes. If you are a linguistic learner, you may need to write and then "say out loud" the steps in a process, the formula, or actions that lead up to a significant event. If you are a kinesthetic learner you may need to use your finger to trace over a diagram to remember it or to "tap out" the steps in solving a problem or "feel" yourself writing or typing the formula.

SCHEDULING STUDY TIME

Effective time management skills are an essential component to your academic success. The more effectively you manage your time the more likely you are to achieve your goals such as completing all of your assignments on time or finishing all of the questions on a unit test or year-end exam. Developing a study schedule helps to ensure you have adequate time to review the subject content and prepare for the exam.

You should review your class notes regularly to ensure you have a clear understanding of the new material. Reviewing your lessons on a regular basis helps you to learn and remember the ideas and concepts. It also reduces the quantity of material that you must study prior to a unit test or year-end exam. If this practice is not part of your study habits, establishing a study schedule will help you to make the best use of your time. The following are brief descriptions of three types of study schedules.

- **LONG-TERM STUDY SCHEDULE** – begins early in the school year or semester and well in advance of an exam; is the **most effective** manner for improving your understanding and retention of the concepts, and increasing self-confidence; involves regular, nightly review of class notes, handouts and text material
- **SHORT-TERM STUDY SCHEDULE** – begins **five to seven days prior to an exam**; must organize the volume of material to be covered beginning with the most difficult concepts; each study session starts with a brief review of what was studied the day before
- **CRAMMING** – occurs the night before an exam; is the **least effective** form of studying or exam preparation; focuses on memorizing and reviewing critical information such as facts, dates, formulas; do not introduce new material; has the potential to increase exam anxiety by discovering something you do not know

Regardless of the type of study schedule you use, you may want to consider the following to maximize your study time and effort:

- establish a regular time and place for doing your studying
- minimize distractions and interruptions during your study time
- plan a ten minute break for every hour that you study
- organize the material so you begin with the most challenging content first

- divide the subject content into smaller manageable "chunks" to review
- develop a marking system for your study notes to identify key and secondary concepts, concepts that you are confident about, those that require additional attention or about which you have questions
- reward yourself for sticking to your schedule and/or completing each review section
- alternate the subjects and type of study activities to maintain your interest and motivation
- make a daily task list with the headings "must do", "should do", and "could do"
- begin each session by quickly reviewing what you studied the day before
- maintain your usual routine of eating, sleeping, and exercising to help you concentrate for extended periods of time

KEY STRATEGIES FOR REVIEWING

Reviewing textbook material, class notes, and handouts should be an ongoing activity and becomes more critical in preparing for exams. You may find some of the following strategies useful in completing your review during your scheduled study time.

READING OR SKIMMING FOR KEY INFORMATION

- Before reading the chapter, preview it by noting headings, charts and graphs, chapter questions.
- Turn each heading and sub-heading into a question before you start to read.
- Read the complete introduction to identify the key information that is addressed in the chapter.
- Read the first sentence of the next paragraph for the main idea.
- Skim the paragraph noting key words, phrases, and information.
- Read the last sentence of the paragraph.
- Repeat the process for each paragraph and section until you have skimmed the entire chapter.
- Read the complete conclusion to summarize each chapter's contents.
- Answer the questions you created.
- Answer the chapter questions.

Creating Study Notes

Mind Mapping or Webbing

- Use the key words, ideas or concepts from your reading or class notes to create a *mind map or web* (a diagram or visual representation of the information). A mind map or web is sometimes referred to as a knowledge map.
- Write the key word, concept, theory or formula in the centre of your page.
- Write and link related facts, ideas, events, and information to the central concept using lines.
- Use colored markers, underlining, or other symbols to emphasize things such as relationships, information of primary and secondary importance.
- The following example of a mind map or web illustrates how this technique can be used to develop an essay.

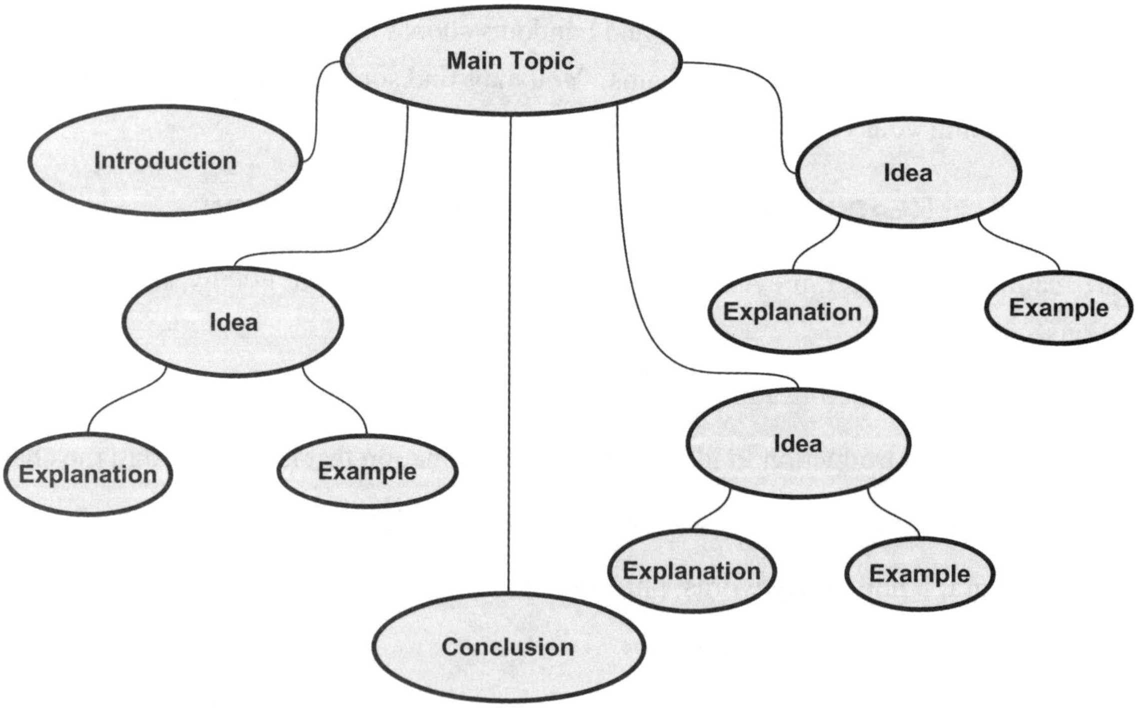

Charts

- Use charts to organize your information and relate theories, concepts, definitions, applications and other important details.
- Collect and enter the information in key categories.
- Use the completed chart as a composite picture of the concept or information.

The following is an example of how a chart can be used to help you organize information when exploring an issue in subjects such as Social Studies, the Sciences, or Humanities.

<table>
<tr><th colspan="6">Define Key Words</th></tr>
<tr><td colspan="6">1.</td></tr>
<tr><td colspan="6">2.</td></tr>
<tr><td colspan="6">3.</td></tr>
<tr><th colspan="6">Explore the Issue</th></tr>
<tr><th colspan="2">Yes to the Issue</th><th colspan="2">No to the Issue</th><th colspan="2">Maybe to the Issue</th></tr>
<tr><td colspan="2">1.</td><td colspan="2">1.</td><td colspan="2">1.</td></tr>
<tr><td colspan="2">2.</td><td colspan="2">2.</td><td colspan="2">2.</td></tr>
<tr><td colspan="2">3.</td><td colspan="2">3.</td><td colspan="2">3.</td></tr>
<tr><th colspan="6">Case Studies and Examples</th></tr>
<tr><td colspan="3">1.</td><td colspan="3">1.</td></tr>
<tr><td colspan="3">2.</td><td colspan="3">2.</td></tr>
<tr><td colspan="3">3.</td><td colspan="3">3.</td></tr>
<tr><th colspan="6">Defense of Your Point of View</th></tr>
<tr><td colspan="6">1.</td></tr>
<tr><td colspan="6">2.</td></tr>
<tr><td colspan="6">3.</td></tr>
</table>

Index Cards

- Write a key event, fact, concept, theory, word or question on one side of the index card.
- On the reverse side, write the date, place, important actions and key individuals involved in the event, significance of the fact, salient features of the concept, essence and application of the theory, definition of the word or answer to the question.
- Use the cards to quickly review important information.

International System of Units (SI)

International System of Units (SI)

SI base unit

Base quantity	Name	Symbol
length	metre	m
mass	kilogram	kg
time	second	s
amount of substance	mole	mol

Derived Measures

Measures	Unit	Symbol
Volume	cubic metre	m^3

SI Prefixes

Factor	Name	Symbol
10^6	mega	*M*
10^3	kilo	*k*
10^{-2}	centi	*c*
10^{-3}	milli	*m*
10^{-6}	micro	μ

Symbols

- Develop your own symbols to use when reviewing your material to identify information you need in preparing for your exam. For example, an exclamation mark (!) may signify something that "must be learned well" because it is a key concept that is likely to appear on unit tests and the year-end exam. A question mark (?) may identify something you are unsure of while a star or asterisk (*) may identify important information for formulating an argument. A check mark (✓) or an (×) can be used to show that you agree or disagree with the statement, sentence or paragraph.

Crib Notes

- Develop brief notes that are a critical summary of the essential concepts, dates, events, theories, formulas, supporting facts, or steps in a process that are most likely to be on the exam.
- Use your crib notes as your "last minute" review before you go in to write your exam. You can not take crib notes into an exam.

MEMORIZING

- **ASSOCIATION** relates the new learning to something you already know. For example, in distinguishing between the spelling of 'dessert' and 'desert', you know 'sand' has only one 's' and so should desert.
- **MNEMONIC DEVICES** are sentences you create to remember a list or group of items. For example, the first letters of the words in the sentence "**E**very **G**ood **B**oy **D**eserves **F**udge" helps you to remember the names of the lines on the treble clef staff (E, G, B, D, and F) in music.
- **ACRONYMS** are words formed from the first letters of the words in a group. For example, **HOMES** helps you to remember the names of Canada's five Great Lakes (**H**uron, **O**ntario, **M**ichigan, **E**rie, and **S**uperior).
- **VISUALIZING** requires you to use your mind's eye to "see" the chart, list, map, diagram, or sentence as it exists in your textbook, notes, on the board, computer screen or in the display.

NOTES

Economic Growth: USA

ECONOMIC GROWTH: USA

Table of Correlations

Topic	Concepts	Related Concepts, Terms, and Facts	Related Questions
CHANGES CAUSED BY INDUSTRIALIZATION	How did industrialization occur and what impact did it have on society? What impact did industrialization have on the United States?	The Industrial Revolution The Agricultural Revolution The Enclosure Movement The Domestic System The Factory System Urbanization Mechanization Specialization Mass production Automation Transportation Immigration Change	1 – 23
THE MARKET ECONOMY	How did the land, labour, and capital influence the market economy?	Land Labour Capital Scarcity The business cycle Corporations The role of entrepreneurs The role of labour The role of government The role of consumers Beliefs and values	24 – 60
QUALITY OF LIFE	How is quality of life influenced by the values and beliefs of the market systems? What changes in the beliefs and values have occurred as a result of industrialization?	Lifestyles resulting from a market economy The social, economic, spiritual, and physical impact of the market system	61 – 62

INDUSTRIALIZATION

Industrialization is an on-going process where societies develop their industrial sectors and involves the movement from a pre-industrialized state to an industrialized state. In Europe during the 18th century, this was largely marked by a change from an agricultural society to an industrial society. Exactly what "industry" means is debatable but conventionally it has been considered as falling into three sectors: primary, secondary, and tertiary. More recently, the fourth term "quaternary" has been added.

Primary industry is essentially the extractive industry including such activities as mining, quarrying and oil extraction. Secondary industry involves the processing of raw materials. Tertiary industry is basically the service industry responsible for distributing the products. And, Quaternary industry is now seen as the knowledge-based or information economy including computer analysis of data and business intelligence, as well as advertising and media creation.

Industrial Revolution

The Industrial Revolution is a term used to describe the extensive changes that took place primarily in Great Britain during the 18th and 19th centuries. Such a view is traditionally "Eurocentric" as many areas of the world underwent changes and restructuring based on textiles, metals, water power, steam power, and transportation. Conventional history texts portray the Industrial Revolution as a spread or diffusion of ideas, inventions, discoveries and industrial processes from Great Britain to Western Europe, and subsequently to North America.

Domestic Factory System

An important aspect of the way of life in the 18th century was the opportunity for women and men to work at home. This was known as the domestic factory system. It is sometimes referred to as the cottage industry. Today, such enterprises would be called home-based businesses. One example of this system was textile production, and primarily the production of wool products. Spinning and weaving took place on the home premises. The Spinning Jenny was used to produce wool that was turned into woollen goods. It was powered by hand or foot-power. For many families, the production process took place upstairs in many of the small, stone built homes. Today, many of these old houses remain in the counties of Lancashire and Yorkshire. The large slatted windows let natural light penetrate into the house allowing the home-makers to see what they were spinning. This reduced the use of candles or oil lamps.

There were many social and community advantages to this system. It allowed parents to look after their children in their homes and to work on the premises. There was a sense of community in small towns and villages. The output from the Spinning Jenny was nowhere as plentiful as the later mechanical machines such as the Power Loom and the Water Frame located in purpose built factories or mills. With competition from these new machines, the fabric of the social and economic system changed. People now had to leave their homes and work in factories owned by businessmen or entrepreneurs. Working conditions were generally more oppressive, lighting conditions were grim and workers now were employed for wages determined by the business owners. Travel from home to factory was now more important and the economic relationships in the communities changed dramatically.

In the USA, the growth of the cotton industry took place in the early 19th century. In New England, the swift streams and the wet, maritime climate allowed the generation of power, which in turn permitted the industry to grow.

With the availability of cotton in the Deep South, together with innovations in machinery, the harnessing of water power, the building of factories and the availability of slaves who "picked a bale of cotton" for their white owners, the cotton industry thrived.

India also had a history of cotton production but at this time Great Britain became the world's powerhouse and dominated the manufacturing of cotton products mainly based on imports of raw cotton from the USA.

Urbanization

The process by which cities grow and spread is termed as urbanization. During Industrial Revolution times in Europe many of the towns and cities were expanding in response to the growth of factories that needed a workforce for industry. Industries began to grow in towns and cities, which in turn, acted as a stimulus for more people to move to the new industries in search of employment. In some areas this resulted in “slums” or poorer areas of housing as described by the writer Charles Dickens in many of his novels. In the USA, where there was more space and relatively less concentrated areas of population, industrial sites were better planned, and cities grew up in response to the need to industrialize.

Mechanization

With new inventions in machinery and steam power, manual labour or animal power was replaced in society. Several inventions dramatically reduced the time taken to produce goods and increased productivity or output. There are many examples of machines that were effective. However, this change meant that the relatively unskilled labourer could replace the traditional craftsperson. These people then could be paid lower wages for goods produced thus increasing profits for the business owners.

Specialization

The act of making something suitable for a specific purpose is known as specialization. It is also the special line of work adopted to achieve a specific purpose. New inventions in engineering were highly specialized during the Industrial Revolution period. Watt, Newcomen, and Boulton all adapted special machine parts in the invention of their steam engines in the late 18th and early 19th centuries. In the coal mines, the use of specialised steam engines resolved the problem of flooding. Eli Whitney's cotton gin, and his production of high quality guns and rifles illustrate the specialization of production techniques as well as products.

Mass Production

Mass production involves producing the same goods quickly and consistently. It aims for the maximum output with the minimum of expense or efficiency. With the conveyor belt and assembly line, people ended up doing the same task over and over again. Eventually, machines replaced labour intensive jobs. Today, robot arms weld car bodies on many production lines where vehicles are mass-produced.

From a historical perspective in the American context, Henry Ford is typical of an entrepreneur associated with mass production. The mass production of large quantities of the same good on an assembly line using standardised designs is reflected in his Model-T Ford. However in the early 1800's, Eli Whitney and his invention of the cotton gin and his work on the production of armaments is largely seen as the trigger for the American Industrial Revolution and mass production. More information is available at http://www.eliwhitney.org/

Eli Whitney is also given credit for inventing standard interchangeable parts for machines and the design of milling machines used in fine metal work. According to various historical sources, Whitney was a true humanitarian, valuing the workers in his factories and treating them fairly. This was in stark contrast to some other factory owners, and may reflect the fact that he rose from a poor background to fame and fortune.

Automation

The replacement of manual operations by machines, and today, by computers, is described as automation. In Industrial Revolution times, many tasks became automated particularly in the textile industries, in the iron and steel foundries, and in the manufacturing sectors. Efficiency and speed are linked with this process. Automation also led to a shift in employment opportunities for people who were displaced from one area to another. Although this led to unemployment, there was significant growth in other sectors of the economy such as the distribution and transportation of goods which provided new employment opportunities.

Transportation

In Europe, much of the impetus for the Industrial Revolution occurred through the revolution in transportation. The inventions of steam power and engineering led to the development of railways, which enabled goods and people to be transported around the country. In Great Britain, the cities expanded rapidly and were linked by railways. In the USA and Canada, where distances are many times greater, cities in the northeastern seaboard were connected to an extensive railway network during the 1850s. By the 1860s construction began on a network which would link the Mid-west to the Pacific Ocean. In Europe, the construction of canals was also significant and barges transported heavy materials such as coal and iron ore to industries. At the same time there was also a rapid expansion in roads construction and turnpikes or toll-roads.

Immigration

Immigration to the USA is a main part of its history. Between 1500 and 1790 waves of Europeans, notably the British immigrants, settled the land that was to become the USA. However, many religious and 'political' groups were also part of the immigration history such as the Pilgrims, Puritans, Royalists, and the Quakers. During this time there were also significant numbers of Germans and Dutch immigrants who settled the eastern seaboard. New Netherlands later became New York and New Jersey.

Between 1710 and 1775, many Scots and Irish also settled North America looking for a better life. Chattel slavery or the slave trade was forced immigration to America, particularly to the southwest states. According to several sources there were over 700, 000 African slaves in the USA by 1790.

Between 1850 and 1930 there was a further wave of German settlers, as well as French-Canadians, Italians and Jews.

Change

Change involves transformation, alteration, and replacement. Changes can be very rapid or very slow. Social scientists and historians have identified major changes in societies and have given them specific period names such as the Enlightenment, the French Revolution, the Industrial Revolution. Internal and external factors can lead to changes and sometimes the word 'growth' is used synonymously with change. When analyzing change, social scientists and historians may use beliefs and values and ask the philosophical question, "Was this change good for society? If so, why?" This then leads to a question about making judgements on the validity of the changes and seeks to address a question of motive. A powerful question is to ask. "Whose interests were or are being served by the change?" The follow-up question is, "And has the change improved things for the better?"

MARKET ECONOMY

The market economy is basically the arrangement where buyers and sellers exchange goods and services for money. This can be a simple exchange such as a garage sale or an extremely sophisticated arrangement of exchange such as the stock market.

Scarcity

The concept of scarcity is one of the basic ideas in economics. It is tied to the notion that all goods and services are limited. For example, the more demand there is for a product the less there will be, unless the supply for that product increases. Because there are limits on most resources, choices must be made in regard to that resource. The price of a product is also reflected by its scarcity. Economic growth is also connected to scarcity. A tension exists between having unlimited economic needs and wants with limited natural and human resources. A resource such as sunlight might be considered as the only unlimited resource.

Factors of Production

Traditionally factors of production are seen as **land**, **labour** and **capital**. That is, physical space, a workforce, and money and investment. Associated with the factors are four main economic questions:

- What goods and services should be produced?
- How should goods and services be produced?
- How should goods and services be distributed?
- Who decides on the allocation of these resources, methods of production and the distribution of goods?

The last question is very important because in a 'free' market economy, the natural conditions of the market place control these factors with business people and investors risking their capital. By contrast, the mixed or command economy is run on different lines, where factors of production are controlled by significant government decisions and government intervention.

Business Cycle

In a market economy, fluctuations in business are affected by supply and demand and are part of a natural, unregulated cycle called the **business cycle**. The cycle is caused by changes in prices for products. A period of rising prices is seen as inflation and a period of falling prices is seen as deflation. The fluctuations in the market make this cycle self-regulatory with peaks and troughs in supply, demand, and prices. Volatility or extremes in this cycle can lead to the economic condition of "boom and bust". For example, in the USA during the 1920's, there was a period of affluence known as the "Roaring Twenties" followed by the dramatic crash of the stock market in the 1930's leading to the "Great Depression" with mass unemployment and poverty.

Corporations

In a market economy, corporations are large companies that usually have operations across the globe. Today, such companies as Microsoft, IBM, Shell, Esso, Ford, Toyota, Nike, General Electric, and Disney are household names across the globe. These companies are now known as multinational corporations and practise a special form of central planning within a competitive market situation. The ultimate aim of a corporation in a capitalist economy or in a free market is seen as global domination from an economic viewpoint. Certainly, the survival of a corporation is based on profitability. At different times in history different companies have dominated the marketplace.

Role of Entrepreneurs

Entrepreneurs are people who are risk takers with money or capital. They invest their money in projects hoping in return to make significant profits. In the USA, Donald Trump has recently become a media icon but he has been a corporate giant in real estate, developing land and constructing buildings in Manhattan, New York. The USA has had a long line of famous entrepreneurs including Henry Ford, John Davidson Rockefeller, J. Paul Getty, Howard Hughes, Mary Kay, and Bill Gates. Many fortunes have been made and lost through good investments and bad investments. A successful entrepreneur is regarded as a person who knows which projects to invest in, in order to make a profit.

Role of Labour

A person agrees to exchange his or her time for a certain amount of money. Similarly, an employer or businessperson wishes to purchase labour from an employee. Theoretically, in a free market economy the employer wants to minimize the amount of money paid to the employee for a set amount of time, whereas the employee wishes to maximize the amount of money for the minimum amount of time.

On the other hand, if a situation exists where work is scarce, the worker may choose or be forced to work for low wages. Conversely, if a worker has special skills that are in high demand or there is a shortage of labour, a worker may be paid very high wages. In this respect, the role of labour can regulate the market place.

Role of Government

The economic thinking predominantly associated with the USA is capitalism with emphasis on *laissez-faire* (leave alone), where the marketplace takes care of itself without government involvement. Adam Smith originally presented this economic theory or policy in his book called *The Wealth of Nations*, written in Great Britain in 1776. Politicians followed this policy during the early part of the industrial revolution but eventually they were forced to intervene by making laws when working conditions in factories and mines became unacceptable.

Governments today, with their immense power, can significantly change the way an economy works, and can regulate supply and demand. They can also tax and spend, and invest where they see fit. Some argue that the role of government in the economy should be minimal, whereas others argue that the government has a major obligation to be involved in economic decisions. It largely depends on the ideology or political system of the country. In the western world, where governments are accountable to the people through democracy, a nation's budget is available and open to citizens so those politicians are accountable for their decisions.

Role of Consumers

In the free market, consumers or people who buy goods and services, have a significant effect on the economy by "dollar voting". That is, using their money to choose to buy or not to buy a certain product. In the former case, where the product is in demand or a high seller, the company will make a profit. Think of Apple's recent iPod. It has been extremely profitable for Apple Computers.

If the product does not sell, sales will be low, and the item will not be profitable. The product may then be discontinued. If a company depends solely on this type of product for economic survival, then in the 'worst case' scenario, the company may become bankrupt or be liquidated.

In this regard, **competition** is seen as a very important regulating factor. It may be seen as a healthy way to ensure that high quality products are sold to the consumer. In the capitalist world, the role of advertizing is very significant in creating demand. The way consumers perceive a product is a critical step in influencing supply and demand. Fads, trends, fashions, peer pressure, and the media are all major ways that advertizers manipulate or persuade the consumer to buy products.

If consumers have little money to spend, then products will not sell, and sales will be low ultimately resulting in "lay-offs" or unemployment. This scenario is sometimes referred to as a **recession**. Because there are more unemployed in society and they have little money to spend, fewer products are sold and the situation worsens. The worst case of this economic situation is a depression such as the hard times experienced in the 1930's in North America and Europe.

In a market economy consumer demand is dramatically affected by **advertizing**. This is a powerful force in "persuading" people to buy products. Product exposure and branding is promoted through various media and communication channels.

Beliefs and Values

Beliefs are ideas or convictions that a person holds and accepts as true. Beliefs also imply a degree of faith that what the person believes is at the essence of what the person does. On the other hand, values are fundamental ideas about what is important in life and can be a standard of conduct by which individuals, groups and nations think, act, and make judgements. Societal values are those shared ideals about what is important, good, and right in society.

Ultimately, the question of which economic system is the best comes down to beliefs and values: what is the best and most effective way for a country to use its resources and provide for its citizens? Should the individual be responsible for his or her economic well being in society without government interference? Or, should the government ensure that controlling the economy and making economic decisions on behalf of society meet the economic well being of its citizenry. Such decisions involve making choices between individualism and collectivism, capitalism and centrally planned economies, and freedom and control.

In the case of the USA, the general perception is that the economy of the country is largely based on the free market, market economy, and capitalist ideals. In this case, entrepreneurs who own and operate businesses, take risks with their money to make profits. The main duty of government is to allow the economy to operate with a minimum of regulation.

The capitalist system can produce **inequalities** where some individuals grow very rich through the market system; while at the same time, there may also be significant numbers of very poor people in society. Students can analyse the different positions that can be taken on inequality and the market system. However, where a free market exists and competition is strong, it is inevitable that there will be "winners and losers."

QUALITY OF LIFE

The quality of life is both an abstract and real term that involves the opportunities that individuals in society have to enjoy lifestyles. It is connected to spiritual, mental, and physical aspects of life as well as social and economic, factors. External and internal conditions and perceptions determine the quality of life. It is also a relative term, and for many, a judgement about the state of well being.

The key difference between the models of economic growth in the USA compared with Canada or the former Soviet Union is the degree of self-sufficiency in determining the quality of life.

In general terms, the "Great American Dream" in the USA places emphasis on individualism, and personal success through hard work and personal initiative. It also tends to support competition as a way of life, and personal responsibility for financial matters.

Social benefits, and in particular health care, is largely the responsibility of the individual or corporations, rather than the government. So users or companies have to pay for these services. Economic inequalities exist in a society based on the market economy and this affects the quality of life. Increasing the standard of living through acquiring wealth provides an incentive for individuals to succeed economically, commercially, and financially.

ECONOMIC GROWTH: USA

CHANGES CAUSED BY INDUSTRIALIZATION

1. The Industrial Revolution stemmed from
   A. rapid scientific progress
   B. modernization of the economy
   C. establishment of overseas trade
   D. increased agricultural efficiency

2. The invention that triggered changes in the textile industry was the
   A. flying shuttle
   B. water frame
   C. spinning jenny
   D. power loom

3. The development of spinning mills resulted in the relocation of the textile industry to
   A. towns
   B. rivers
   C. ports
   D. mines

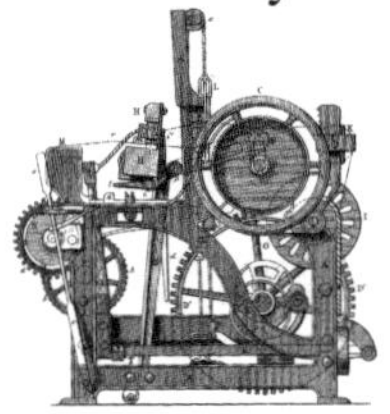

4. In the United States, early industry was located in the New England region because it was close to
   A. European markets
   B. raw materials
   C. water power
   D. transport

Use the information below to answer questions 5 to 9.

Farming in the 1700s

Prior to the 18th century, land in England had been cultivated under the "open field system." Farmland was divided into three fields – one field was planted in the spring; one was planted in the fall; and the last was allowed to lie fallow (unused). Each villager was allotted numerous strips of land scattered over the surrounding countryside. This resulted in a very inefficient system. Much time was wasted travelling from one field to another.

In addition, the strips were too small and too scattered to allow farmers to use machinery or even plow their fields easily. As a result, the fields were often over-planted or over-grazed, and productivity was low. Most farmers produced barely enough to survive and had little time for developing new and more effective farming techniques.

5. The term *productivity* refers to the
   A. type of crops grown by each farmer
   B. length of time it took each farmer to plant his fields
   C. amount that was grown or raised by each farmer
   D. number of animals each farmer possessed

6. Farming prior to the 18th century was inefficient mainly due to the
   A. heavy taxes levied on each farmer
   B. small size and scattered nature of the farm-holdings
   C. inefficient use of machinery
   D. lack of education of the average farmer

7. *Subsistence agriculture* dominated prior to the 18th century. This means that most of each farmer's production was

   A. sold locally

   B. intended for export

   C. taken by the government in the form of taxes

   D. consumed by the farmer and his family

8. A factor that **most likely** caused farmers to continue farming the same way they always had was the

   A. high rents charged by landlords for the use of the land

   B. decline in soil fertility

   C. unwillingness of the farmers to try new techniques due to fear of failure

   D. low level of mechanization of the farms

9. The eventual result of the type of production depicted in the reading was the

   A. development of overseas trade

   B. enclosure of farmers' fields

   C. development of improved varieties of grain

   D. increase in the number of small farmers

Use the following information to answer questions 10 to 14.

Factors Influencing Industrialization in England

1. Increased agricultural efficiency
2. A surplus of labour
3. Rapid population growth
4. Innovations in manufacturing techniques
5. A strong entrepreneurial class
6. Internal unity
7. Political stability
8. Improvements in transportation
9. An overseas empire
10. Abundant supplies of coal and iron

10. The two factors that were **most** important in establishing a market for the goods produced by England during the Industrial Revolution were factors

    A. 2 and 4

    B. 3 and 9

    C. 6 and 7

    D. 5 and 8

CHALLENGER QUESTION

11. England's potential rivals in industrial development, Italy and Germany, were divided into numerous independent states. The two factors that reflect England's advantages over its rivals are factors

    A. 8 and 9

    B. 4 and 5

    C. 6 and 7

    D. 2 and 9

12. By the middle of the 19th century, different regions of England were joined together by a network of improved roads, a comprehensive system of canals, and a growing railway system. These features relate to factor

    A. 4

    B. 6

    C. 8

    D. 9

13. Much of England's success was because of the large number of skilled inventors and innovators who did much to push England to the forefront in industrial production. This is best reflected in factors

    A. 2, 6, and 10

    B. 1, 4, and 5

    C. 3, 6, and 9

    D. 1, 5, and 8

CHALLENGER QUESTION

14. The development of the iron industry was critical in England's industrial development. This is **best** reflected by factor

A. 2

B. 3

C. 5

D. 10

Use the information below to answer questions 15 to 19.

Reading 1: Charles Townshend
Townshend's innovation was the development of the four-field system of crop rotation. Under the old three-field system, one field was always lying fallow and, therefore, unproductive. With four fields always in production, agricultural output could be doubled. In addition, with the growing of fodder crops, animals could be kept through the winter instead of being slaughtered in the fall.

Reading 2: Jethro Tull
Tull's contribution to agriculture was the seed drill. Prior to Tull's invention, fields were planted by broadcast sowing. The seed was simply scattered on the ground by hand. This meant that the seed was planted unevenly resulting in wasted space in some parts of the field and overcrowding of plants in others. The seed drill planted each seed evenly, ensuring each plant had an equal chance of success.

Reading 3: Robert Bakewell
Bakewell applied to domestic animals the same breeding techniques that had been used for centuries to develop a variety of dogs and horses. The results were impressive. In 1701, the average ox weighed 170 kg, the average sheep 17 kg, and the average calf 23 kg. By 1800, the average size of all of these animals had more than doubled. This greatly increased the amount of food available from livestock.

15. An important result of all of these developments in English agriculture was the increased

A. variety of crops grown in England

B. supply of food

C. cost of food produced in England

D. amount of available farm land

16. Together, these and other developments resulted in a marked change in English farming known as the

A. Agricultural Revolution

B. Scientific Revolution

C. Age of Machines

D. Commercial Revolution

17. A trend that accompanied these developments into the late 20th century was

A. increased cost of farm production

B. the reduction in the size of farms

C. a decrease in the number of farmers

D. a decline in soil fertility

18. Without these agricultural developments, industrialization in England would have suffered from a

A. lack of overseas markets

B. weak domestic market

C. shortage of food for the growing population

D. low demand for agricultural machinery

CHALLENGER QUESTION

19. The stimulus for many of the innovations was high prices for agricultural products. Prices remained high during **most** of the 18th and early 19th centuries mainly because of the

A. disruption of the trade between England and its overseas colonies

B. protection of domestic markets by high tariffs

C. government subsidies paid to large farmers

D. rapid population growth and almost unbroken war in Europe

20. During the 19th Century, entrepreneurs in the United States benefitted by

A. low taxes on imported goods

B. an advanced transportation system

C. protection from foreign competition

D. a government opposed to government involvement in business

21. A key technological development in utilizing the huge resource potential of the United States was the

A. building of railroads

B. invention of the riverboat

C. construction of canals

D. development of coastal shipping

22. Given the size of the United States, a key development in its industrialization was the

A. creation of the Pony express

B. construction of the first transcontinental railroad

C. improvements in Atlantic ports

D. construction of the Panama canal

23. The term ***trigger industry*** refers to an industry that

A. associates with the development of armaments

B. stimulates many other economic activities

C. dominates one sector of the economy

D. other enterprises attempt to copy

THE MARKET ECONOMY

Use the following information to answer questions 24 to 29.

Case Study 1
Jim Flobber reluctantly closed and locked the door of his small hardware store for the last time. He sighed. It had been a decent living for 15 years, but then that huge chain store had moved in only three blocks away. Folks that used to come to his store drove right by on their way to the megastore. There was absolutely no way that he could survive.

Case Study 2
Mrs. Ko and her husband arrived in Canada in 1986. They both acquired jobs as kitchen helpers. By 1989, they had saved enough to open a small restaurant of their own. In 1993, they started a janitorial service and expanded their restaurant. By 1998, their two businesses employed 25 people and brought in a clear profit of $200,000 per year. When interviewed by a local newspaper about her amazing success, Mrs. Ko said, "It's not hard to make money in Canada, you just have to work."

Case Study 3
Bob Apples noticed that in the last two years a large number of small landscaping businesses had opened up. Believing he was entering an expanding market, Bob spent his life's savings on a pickup truck and landscaping equipment. The business, however, did not take off as expected. He found that even when he offered discount rates there was not much need for his services. The problem was that there were simply too many other people doing the same thing.

Case Study 4
"The problem with snowblowers," said Bill Clarke, "is that all they do is blow snow. The rest of the year, they just sit. I have developed a machine that can blow snow in the winter, rototill gardens in the spring, and mow lawns in the summer. My machine costs only 20% more than a single snowblower. So far, I have two big lawnmower firms bidding for the rights to my invention."

Case Study 5
Frank Chan counted out the day's receipts. Another pretty good day. He had been quite concerned when that gigantic discount store had moved into town two years ago. But he had found a way to compete. The big store could always outdo him for prices, but big stores don't repair their products when they break. He had simply gone into the appliance and machine repair business. He had even contacted the manager of the big store to let him know what he was doing. The discount store sent him a lot of business. It was easier for the big store to let Frank repair its defective merchandise than to set up its own repair shop.

CHALLENGER QUESTION

24. The principle of the market economy that is illustrated in case study 1 is

A. supply and demand

B. competition

C. individualism

D. private ownership of the means of production

25. The free enterprise characteristics of *innovation* and *adaptation* are illustrated in case studies

A. 2 and 3 **B.** 3 and 4

C. 4 and 5 **D.** 1 and 2

26. The free market principle of rewarding hard work is **most clearly** illustrated in case study

A. 1 **B.** 2

C. 3 **D.** 4

27. The result of an oversupply of goods or services is illustrated in case study

A. 1 **B.** 2

C. 3 **D.** 4

CHALLENGER QUESTION

28. A principle of free enterprise that is illustrated by case study 2 is

A. supply and demand

B. public ownership

C. freedom of choice

D. individual initiative

29. In response to a decline in the value of the Canadian dollar, a government that believes in the values of the market economy would

A. increase taxes to create a budget surplus

B. allow the dollar to fall until it stops falling by itself

C. raise interest rates to encourage foreigners to buy Canadian dollars

D. lower interest rates to encourage foreigners to sell Canadian dollars

30. In a market economy, the main duty of government is to

A. establish appropriate environmental standards

B. prevent the creation of monopolies

C. provide services for the poor

D. allow the economy to operate with a minimum of regulation

31. In a private enterprise system, low prices, high quality, and innovation are normally a result of

A. private ownership of land

B. individual initiative

C. consumerism

D. competition

32. The man considered to be the **most** important theorist of the market economy is

A. John D. Rockefeller

B. Charles Hall

C. Adam Smith

D. Ray Kroc

CHALLENGER QUESTION

33. The owners of a modern corporation consist of

A. all members of the Board of Directors

B. all of the workers in the company

C. all members of the public who own shares in the company

D. all workers and all members of the board of Directors

34. The role of the consumer in a private enterprise economy is to

A. provide the demand for products in order to stimulate the economy

B. insure that consumer goods are of good quality

C. make sure that levels of competition are maintained

D. regulate levels of production

CHALLENGER QUESTION

35. In a model market economy, interest rates are determined by

A. a government regulated central bank

B. a number of private banks working together

C. the rate at which the central bank prints money

D. public demand for credit

Use the information below to answers questions 36 to 40.

Speaker 1
"It is difficult to imagine a system closer to perfection than the market economy. It functions without any central directive, so no complex government apparatus is needed. It creates an economic environment that ensures high quality, low prices, and a constant stream of new ideas. It rewards hard work and intelligence and insures a high standard of living for all members of society."

Speaker 2
"It is true that the market system is capable of creating great wealth and a rapidly expanding economy. However, the market system also creates problems of over-consumption and pollution. A great deal of waste is created by the desire for the great quantities of useless products."

Speaker 3
"The capitalist system is not without its defects. Many people can grow rich through the market system, but that wealth is not evenly distributed. For every millionaire there are hundreds of desperately poor people who are barely surviving."

Speaker 4
"The laissez-faire economy distorts societal values. Some athletes and movie stars are paid huge salaries, while more important members of society, such as doctors, scientists, teachers, and police are relatively poorly paid."

Speaker 5
"Of course the market economy results in inequality. But is that necessarily a bad thing? Why should all people be paid the same? Do all people work equally hard? Do all people make an equal contribution to society? Are all people equally gifted or intelligent? What a dull world it would be if everyone was economically equal."

36. The point of disagreement among the speakers is over whether or not the market economy

A. should be regulated

B. creates an unfair system

C. results in unfair pricing

D. produces too many goods

37. That the market economy encourages people to buy products that they do not really need is a belief held by speaker

A. 1

B. 2

C. 3

D. 4

38. That inequality is a good thing is a belief held by speaker

A. 2

B. 3

C. 4

D. 5

39. That capitalism creates a culture that encourages people to adopt harmful attitudes is a belief held by speaker

A. 1

B. 2

C. 4

D. 5

40. That the private enterprise economy is as close to perfection as an economic system can get is a belief held by speaker

A. 1

B. 2

C. 4

D. 5

Use the information below to answer questions 41 to 45.

Speaker 1
"A serious problem of the market economy is its dependence on advertising. Consumers are bombarded with every sort of lie imaginable in order to influence their buying habits. As a result, advertising fails in its most important objective – to inform the public, as the average person does not know what is true and what is false."

Speaker 2
"Without advertising there wouldn't be a modern market economy. Can you imagine trying to learn about new products by word of mouth? It would be impossible. There are simply too many new products on the market for the average person to keep track of. Advertising is the only way to send this information to the buying public."

Speaker 3
"Advertising performs several essential services in the modern private enterprise economy. First, it alerts consumers to the availability of new products. Second, it allows the manufacturers of a new product to produce large quantities of new product because they know that they will be able to sell what they produce. Third, it creates competition between producers of goods and services."

Speaker 4
"A considerable amount of advertising is nothing more than a serious attempt to manipulate the public. Numerous products are presented to the public as being desirable and useful, when in fact they are neither. As a matter of fact, many heavily advertised products such as chewing gum, tobacco, and alcohol are either absolutely useless or downright dangerous."

Speaker 5
"The modern market economy is an economic system based on waste, in which advertising does its part in promoting waste. Consumers are encouraged to buy numerous single use items or products that are packaged in environmentally unfriendly throwaway containers. They are also encouraged to consume large amounts of declining resources."

41. An example of the sort of waste that is the concern of speaker 5 would be

A. oil and gas consumption

B. use of hydroelectric power

C. the purchase of solar panels

D. consumption of grain products such as bread

CHALLENGER QUESTION

42. That advertising makes modern mass production possible is a belief held by speaker

A. 1

B. 2

C. 3

D. 5

43. The speakers who believe that advertising distorts the truth are

A. speakers 1 and 2

B. speakers 3 and 4

C. speakers 1 and 4

D. speakers 2 and 3

44. The speaker who believes that advertising encourages unhealthy habits is speaker

A. 1

B. 2

C. 3

D. 4

45. The speaker who believes that new products would be more expensive without advertising is speaker

A. 1

B. 2

C. 3

D. 5

Use the information below to answer questions 46 to 50.

Advantages of the Market Economy

I. Consumers can influence the goods and services produced.
II. A wide variety of goods and services is available.
III. There are incentives to use resources efficiently.
IV. The economy is flexible.
V. Competition results in high quality, low prices, and innovation.
VI. Monetary rewards encourage people to work harder and produce more.

46. An opponent of the market economy would object to advantage III by pointing out that

A. prices rise as resources become more scarce

B. businesses often find new ways to use resources

C. bulk buying of food and other items has become more common

D. waste disposal has become a major problem in many capitalist nations

47. Which of the above advantages is **closest** to the democratic principle of freedom of choice?

A. I

B. II

C. IV

D. VI

48. An example of how advantage III would work would be

A. an increase in the price of any scarce commodity

B. increased exploration for any scarce mineral

C. hoarding of limited supplies of any product

D. fluctuations in food prices caused by seasonal change

CHALLENGER QUESTION

49. An example of advantage IV would be the

A. world recession caused by higher oil prices in the 1970s

B. switch to alternative fuels caused by an increase in the price of oil in the 1970s

C. increase in the popularity of gas fireplaces

D. development of new uses for petroleum products

50. A critic of the market economy would point out that advantage VI encourages

A. people in a market economy to place acquisition of money above all else

B. members of a market economy to value hard work

C. workers in a market economy to show loyalty to their employers

D. employers in a market economy to reward success

Use the information below to answer questions 51 to 55.

Disadvantages of the Market Economy

- **I.** Advertising manipulates consumers.
- **II.** Social values may be distorted.
- **III.** The economy is subject to the boom and bust cycle.
- **IV.** There are great differences in wealth.
- **V.** Large businesses distort the free market system.

51. An example of disadvantage II would be

- **A.** rewarding those who work hard
- **B.** allowing consumers freedom of choice
- **C.** larger salaries paid to professional athletes
- **D.** rewarding developers of new products

52. A supporter of the market system would disagree with disadvantage V by pointing out that

- **A.** businesses only grow large if they provide what consumers want
- **B.** large businesses have the capacity to eliminate smaller competitors
- **C.** large business can get raw materials more cheaply
- **D.** government controls can slow business growth

53. An example of disadvantage I would be

- **A.** the promotion of outdoor sports such as skiing
- **B.** alerting consumers to a sale
- **C.** introducing a new product to consumers
- **D.** mass marketing of consumer goods such as soft drinks

54. A supporter of the market economy would justify disadvantage IV by pointing out that

- **A.** some members of society inherit their wealth
- **B.** not all members of society harm the environment
- **C.** some members of society contribute more than others
- **D.** certain members of society deserve to be poor

55. To the average member of a market economy, the **most** serious concern would be disadvantage

- **A.** I
- **B.** II
- **C.** III
- **D.** IV

56. The **most** important advantage that large corporations have over other types of businesses is they

- **A.** face less competition than other businesses
- **B.** can raise large sums of money more easily
- **C.** have greater access to raw materials
- **D.** can crush their competitors

CHALLENGER QUESTION

57. A supporter of the market economy would propose that the problem of unemployment be dealt with by

    A. setting up a manpower retraining program

    B. providing financial support until the economy can be improved

    C. placing the unemployed in government run labour camps

    D. having the unemployed take what jobs are available until the economy improves

Use the cartoon below to answer questions 58 and 59.

"If we pay them starvation wages—why do they need a lunch break?"

58. The scene depicted in the cartoon would be **most** typical of a

A. market economy

B. traditional economy

C. command economy

D. mixed economy

CHALLENGER QUESTION

59. A person who favours a *laissez-faire* system would suggest dealing with the situation by

    A. letting the demand for labour determine the wage of workers

    B. instituting a food bank program

    C. promoting minimum wage legislation

    D. advocating the formation of unions

Use the following information to answer question 60.

In 1998, *The Edmonton Sun* newspaper celebrated its twentieth anniversary. Since its inception, the newspapers' total revenue has increased 400%. General manager David Black credits the success of the newspaper to people power. "I've always said it's the dedication of the employees that has made this paper what it is today. Everyone is always looking for ways to improve the paper."

60. The speaker attributes the success of *The Edmonton Sun* to which factor of production commonly found in a market economy?

A. Capital

B. Land

C. Labour

D. Mass production

QUALITY OF LIFE

Use the cartoon below to answer question 61.

"Henderson......you have a fine arts degree. How would you arrange the pepperoni and mushrooms?"

61. A weakness of the market economy illustrated by the cartoon is that

- **A.** people are limited in how much money they can make
- **B.** people can apply for any job they want
- **C.** people find work that is appropriate to their training
- **D.** people are frequently take jobs that they are over-qualified for

Use the cartoon below to answer question 62.

"Well, it's American-made after your child assembles it."

62. The cartoon refers to the issue in market economies of

- **A.** consumer products being produced by foreign labour, instead of domestic labour
- **B.** the lack of production of domestic goods in local economy
- **C.** the lack of high quality goods available in the marketplace
- **D.** the exploitation of child labour used to create inexpensive goods

NOTES

Economic Growth: Former USSR

Former USSR

ECONOMIC GROWTH: FORMER USSR

Table of Correlations

Topic	Concepts	Related Concepts, Terms, and Facts	Related Questions
GEOGRAPHY HAS GREATLY INFLUENCED THE GROWTH OF RUSSIA	How has the geography of Russia influenced its economic development?	Location Physical features Climate Vegetation Natural Resources Area Population distribution	1 – 8
CHANGES CAUSED BY INDUSTRIALIZATION	Industrialization in pre-Revolutionary Russia	Economic conditions in Russia prior to 1917 Russian society prior to 1917 Serfdom Agrarian society	9 – 10
GOVERNMENT PLANNING INFLUENCED SOVIET ECONOMIC DEVELOPMENT		The 1917 Revolution Economic planning The New Economic Policy Collectives Five-Year Plans	11 – 29
THE CENTRALLY PLANNED ECONOMY	How are land, labour, and capital controlled by government?	The role of government The role of consumers The role of labour Centralization of authority Beliefs and values Collectivism Equality Individualism Security Freedom of choice Needs versus wants	30 – 61
QUALITY OF LIFE	How has the quality of life been influenced by the values and beliefs associated with central planning?	Lifestyles resulting from a centrally planned system The social, economic, spiritual, and physical impact of central planning	62 – 66

GEOGRAPHY

- Location
- Landforms
- Bodies of water
- Climate
- Vegetation
- Natural resources
- Size
- Population distribution

It is important that students can identify both physical and human features of the former USSR available from a variety of sources including Atlases, maps, graphs and tables. At this level, it is also important that students are able to make connections between different variables and geographic factors, and develop an understanding of how the physical world impacts on the human environment. Good, up to date information is available from the CIA World Factbook that is available on line at http://www.cia.gov/cia/publications/factbook/

There are many similarities between the former USSR and Canada in terms of the physical environment: a northern country, an extensive land mass, similar ranges of daylight, similar climatic regions, several large lakes and water bodies, similar soil types, similar natural resources, oil and mineral reserves, and similar engineering challenges.

In terms of the human characteristics, the former USSR is significantly different from Canada in terms of its beliefs and ideas, culture, cities, occupations, settlement, and population distribution. However, there are some commonalities. For example, Ukrainians who were not unfamiliar with the climate, soils, and agricultural opportunities that were similar to their homeland settled the prairies in Canada. Also Canada and Russia are northern neighbours and this is apparent with the view of the earth from the North Pole or polar projection.

The physical regions and landforms of the former USSR include: the Great Russian Plain, Ural Mountains, West Siberian Plain, Central Siberian Plateau, Caucasus Mountains, Turan Lowlands, Ural Mountains, Far Eastern Highland, and Southeastern Mountains. Each area or mountain area has its distinct characteristics and students should be familiar with their general characteristics.

INDUSTRIALIZATION

- 1917 Revolution
- New Economic Policy – Lenin
- Collectives
- Five-Year Plans – Stalin
- Economic Planning in the post-Stalin Era

1917 Revolution

In February 1917, the Russian workers or 'proletariat' demonstrated against Czar Nicholas II and his aristocratic associates (bourgeoisie) about government decisions. In October 1917, the Bolsheviks, led by Lenin were responsible for overthrowing the government and replacing it with a Communist government. There were many reasons for the revolution but most would agree that it was a period when the people were largely dissatisfied with the standard of living for the average Russian citizen and peasant. Food shortages, factory unrest, lack of power, lack of representation and land ownership, were among the factors that led to civil strife, as well as new political ideas of equality based on the writings of Karl Marx and Fredrich Engels.

Communism

Communism is an economic and political system based on the common ownership of wealth, property and means of production with each person working towards the common good of the state, based on the ability to give and receive according to need. Generally, communism refers to the classless society where economic equality is created by common ownership. In this is process it is necessary for the wealthy classes or bourgeoisie to be (violently) overthrown to achieve this end. The Russian Revolution was based on this belief, and the Communist Party ruled the Soviet Union from 1917 to 1991.

New Economic Policy – Vladimir Lenin

Lenin (his given name was Vladimir Ilich Ulyanov) introduced the New Economic Policy or NEP in 1921 to allow a small amount of decision-making and private enterprise to be held by the Bolsheviks. There had been violent protests about the previous policy of War Communism where the Bolshevik government forced peasants to give food to city workers and the army. Simply stated, the idea of communal ownership or collective ownership did not completely work because citizens also wanted some personal gain and could not rely on the state for everything. It was hoped that this might spark economic development and most historians would agree that the mixing of private enterprise with state economy was somewhat successful until Stalin's rule.

Collectives – Joseph Stalin

The introduction of collectives or **collectivization** was a policy of Joseph Stalin whereby small and medium-scale privately owned farms were taken by the state and turned into larger centrally-planned enterprises during the 1920s and 1930s. One of the reasons for this move towards **nationalization** of farms was that the Soviet Union had to export large amounts of grain and minerals out of the country to pay for foreign-made machinery that was necessary to industrialize. This was part of the Five-Year Plans.

In 1932-33, a huge famine was created in the Soviet Union by a combination of factors including collectivization. Records show that over six million people in the Ukraine starved to death. The forced collectivization was especially hard on the 'Kulaks' or richer peasants, and those that resisted state control were either shot or deported to labour camps.

Five-Year Plans – Joseph Stalin

In 1926, long-range and intermediate economic planning commenced under Stalin. This culminated in a series of economic plans that were implemented in 1928 whereby the development of heavy industry in the Soviet Union was to be targeted. This included the growth of steel, coal, machinery, energy, chemical and military sectors. All means of production were controlled by the state. The results of these plans were that by 1955 the Soviet Union was the second largest industrial power. One criticism of the plans, however, was that the book-keeping and reporting by various groups of individuals were forged or inaccurately reported to meet with production targets set by the state. Nevertheless, the growth of cities and heavy industries in the Soviet Union by the 1950s was remarkable but it came at the cost of individual freedom, extreme hardship for some, and fear of the authorities.

CENTRALLY PLANNED ECONOMY

Scarcity

The concept of scarcity is one of the basic ideas in economics. It is tied to the notion that all goods and services are limited especially when demand is high. In a centrally planned economy, the factors associated with scarcity can be controlled by state intervention. The ability of the government to control the market along with the various factors of production **means that the economy can be controlled and regulated** more readily in this environment than in a free market economy.

Factors of Production

Land, labour, and capital are tightly controlled by the state in a command economy. The state is often equated with an elite, centralized group of politicians and under the Communist Party this was known as the Politburo. It was the most powerful decision-making body of the party. In a command or centrally planned economy provided by the former USSR, this elite group controlled the factors of production.

Role of Government

The Soviet system, prior to the break up of the former USSR, was based on the system of government called the 'socialist state' where everyone was represented equally. Many textbooks show the complex organizational structure of the Soviet government. In practice, the government structure translated into power held by the elites of the Communist Party. Under Stalin, and many other Soviet leaders, power was maintained through brutality, fear, propaganda, and the secret police. Power politics involved crushing any form of dissent and any beliefs other than the 'party line' were strongly discouraged.

After Stalin's death in 1953, the system changed slightly, but with the Cold War and nuclear tension between east and west, the use of fear, repression and harsh consequences for dissenters never really changed until the post-Gorbachev era. The power of the Communist Party was such that it controlled most economic and political decisions until its influence was restricted under Gorbachev. Mikhail Gorbachev came to power as the president in 1985 and brought in *Glasnost* or greater openness with the policy of *Perestroika* or rebuilding or restructuring Soviet society in 1987. He wanted to improve people's living standards through economic reforms. This government measure caused a significant change in thinking in Russian society eventually leading to opening up the former USSR to new economic thinking, policies and trade.

Role of Consumers

In Soviet society during the pre-Gorbachev era, consumer choices were very limited. What little extra money the majority of citizens had from their wages was largely spent on basic needs including food and clothing. Line-ups were a common site. Conditions for the average person were 'basic' and 'western' goods were not available except on the 'black market'. Today, the society in Russia has evolved to a market economy with a wide variety of consumer options and choices of goods from around the world including McDonalds and Starbucks. Russians refer to this new period as "the Restoration".

Role of Labour

The totalitarian state indoctrinated people into the notion of working hard for the good of the country and communism. Many propaganda films showed Stalin working in the fields along side his fellow citizens, and 'Heroes of Labour' were given special elevation in Soviet society. Hard work was highly prized politically, and was satirized by George Orwell in *Animal Farm* where the horse Boxer represents the hard working citizen who is eventually discarded when he is no longer useful for work. One of the features of the former USSR under Stalin, was its relatively large population available as a labour force on farms and in industries. But critics saw this as a weakness of the system where people were discarded by the state when they were no longer capable of work.

Centralization

The process whereby a small, centralized group makes decisions that are then passed outwards is associated with the command economy. It can be likened to dropping a pebble in a pond and watching the ripples spread out. Under the iron rule of dictators or Soviet presidents, many economic decisions were made centrally in this manner and targets were set for economic development. This process involved the maximum amount of control over the economy.

Belief and values

The key belief in this type of economic system is that the state owns the wealth, property and means of production so that each person works for the common good, according to ability, and therefore receives according to need. Underlying this is the notion of equality where everyone is equal in society. The idea of public enterprise also involves collectivism where there is equitable distribution of wealth and income.

ECONOMIC CHANGE

Attempts at Economic Reform

The modern history of the former USSR since the early 20th century is one characterized by dramatic changes in politics and economics. From the overthrow of the Czars, to the communist revolution, to the rise of Lenin, to Stalin's harsh economic policies. From the Cold War, and the rise of the reformers, to the Gorbachev era, to the modified market economy of today under President Putin.

Gorbachev's Reforms

Glasnost is a term that was used by former President Mikhail Gorbachev to describe the era of 'openness' that took place in the former Soviet Union under his leadership during the late 1980s and early 1990s.

During the early part of his presidency and the 'pre-Gorbachev era' severe restrictions were placed by the USSR on contact and trade with the non-Communist world. The communists believed that the capitalist ideology posed a severe threat to the communist world, and the capitalists believed that the communist ideology posed a severe threat to the capitalist world. This clash of beliefs, doctrines and ideologies led to the 'Cold War' and could have resulted in nuclear annihilation particularly over the 'Bay of Pigs' incident involving the stationing of Russian nuclear missiles in Cuba.

Introduction of a Modified Market Economy

Perestroika is a term that was used by former President Mikhail Gorbachev to describe the era of economic and political reforms that took place in the former Soviet Union under his leadership during the late 1980s and early 1990s. The term means 'restructuring' and during this time there was a marked shift away from a centrally planned or command economy toward a mixed economy.

Gorbachev saw that the former USSR could not exist in economic isolation. This view, together with the emergence of a multiparty political system, dramatically changed the fabric of the Soviet Union. Arguably, this action was one of the factors that eventually led to the collapse or break up of the USSR.

Today, the market economy has dramatically changed the economy of the former USSR and recently there has been the rise of the 'gangster' class. In addition a group of 'oligarchs' or very powerful individuals are seen by some as a corrupt, wealthy elite whose personal fortunes have been made by investment in the black market, the underground economy, and other illegal enterprises. Certain key businessmen and entrepreneurs have been arrested by the state for these illegal activities, notably Mikhail Khodorkovsky who has made his fortune in the oil industry and is reputedly one of the richest men in Russia.

Influence of the Global Marketplace

Since the collapse of the Soviet Union in 1991-1992, and the end of the centrally controlled "command economy," the countries that were formerly part of Soviet Union have invited certain business from around the world to compete in their marketplaces. At the same time, life for many citizens has not improved. Some people still struggle to survive, sometimes below the subsistence level without purchasing power. However, for others, the standard of living has dramatically improved in the last ten years.

Many Russians still blame former President Boris Yeltsin and his Prime Minister, Viktor Chernomyrdin for the economic situation that exists today. Crucial to the transition to a market economy was the transfer of business enterprises from state to private ownership. Under Yeltsin, many state owned companies in the oil, gas, automobile, and banking sectors were given as 'gifts' of the Yeltsin government to certain individuals in return for political support.

Today, many multinational companies are part of the Russian economy including McDonalds and Ford. There are also foreign owned oil, agricultural companies and financial institutions in Russia that are taking advantage of the new economy.

According to recent news reports, the McDonalds chain now employs 17,000 Russians in 37 cities and plans to open 25 restaurants this year, mostly in Moscow and St. Petersburg, and 75 more by 2007. It is interesting to note that the McDonalds Corporation is now considered to be reputedly the largest corporate landowner in Russia.

QUALITY OF LIFE

In the former Soviet Union, the quality of life for the everyday person has been highly variable, just as it has been in the "western democracies." Students may like to analyse the differences for different people at different times. The objective of producing a society based on equality was the goal but it may not have ever been reached. It is difficult to generalize.

Certainly, under Czarism, some peasants had poor living conditions whereas some did quite well. During the Russian revolution, living conditions were difficult. Under Stalin, atrocious living conditions were produced with the purges and the famines for different ethnic and regional groups. During the Cold War, consumerism was limited and many wanted to escape from the clutches of communism to go to the free west. Lining up for basic goods and services was the norm. *Glasnost* and *Perestroika* had the objective of improving the quality of life for citizenry. The collapse of the Soviet Union and its break up posed special economic problems for different republics and regions. Today, the new market economy has taken hold.

Students may be given a variety of sources where they have to make judgements about the quality of life for the average Russian and share their reflections on the political systems, past and present. For example, students may have to determine the political and economic viewpoint(s) held by a number of speakers, and decide whether the former USSR has benefited from change.

ECONOMIC GROWTH: FORMER USSR

THE INFLUENCE OF GEOGRAPHY ON THE ECONOMIC DEVELOPMENT OF RUSSIA

Use the following graphs to answer questions 1 to 3.

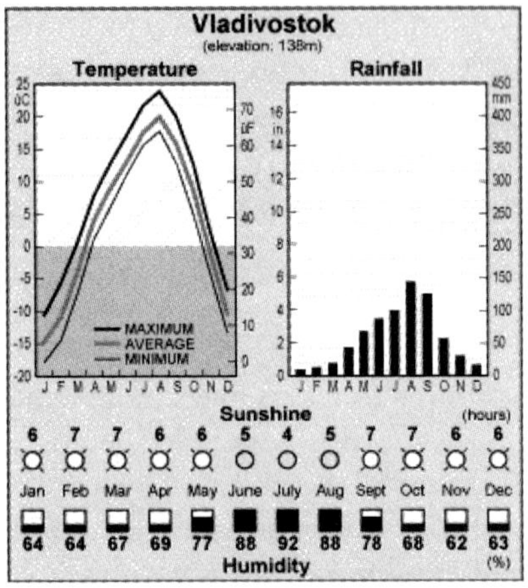

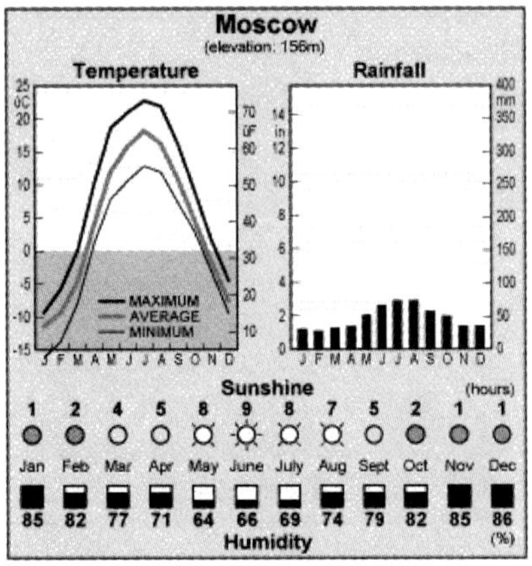

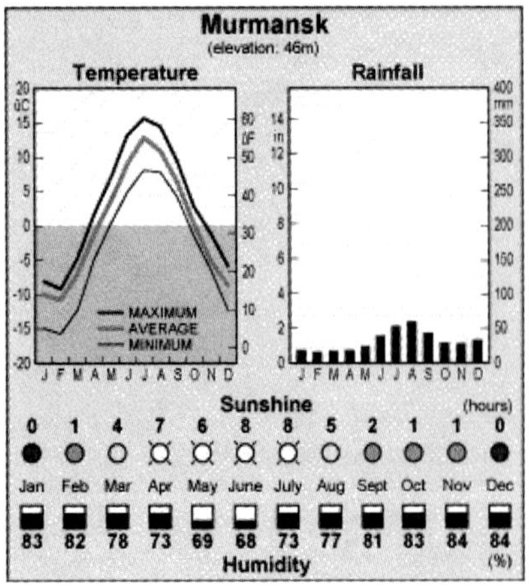

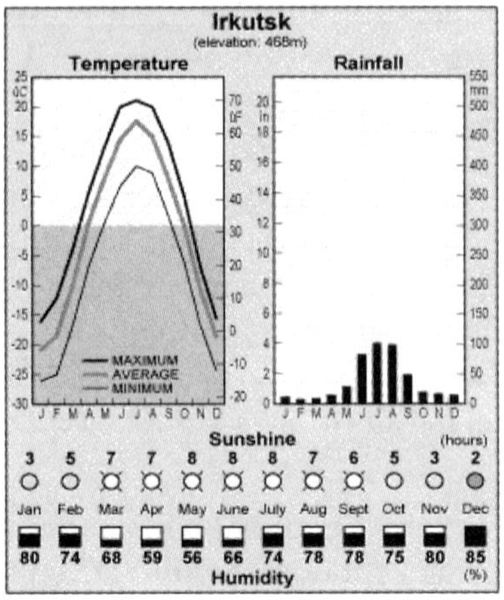

1. Based on the information in the graphs, a general problem of settlement in Russia is the country's

   A. extremely dry climate

   B. relatively short growing season

   C. lack of protective snowfall in winter

   D. low elevation

2. Of the four geographic areas represented by the graphs, the one that is probably **least** suitable for settlement is

   A. Murmansk

   B. Moscow

   C. Vladivostok

   D. Irkutsk

3. Overall, the site that is **most** suitable for settlement is

   A. Murmansk

   B. Moscow

   C. Vladivostok

   D. Irkutsk

CHALLENGER QUESTION

4. The main reason that Russia's population is concentrated in its western regions is that the west
   - **A.** has most of the country's natural resources
   - **B.** is closest to Western Europe
   - **C.** is the least open to invasion
   - **D.** has the most suitable land for agriculture

Use the information below to answer questions 5 to 8.

Source 1
Russia's huge size has hindered its development by making it very difficult for one part of the country to communicate with the other. Few other nations on Earth have had to deal with such vast distances when considering the construction of roads and railroads. It is a problem that concerns Russia even today.

Source 2
The immense area of the Russian nation has provided the country with vast amounts of resources. There is no nation on Earth with such huge resource potential. The only difficulty faced by the Russians in dealing with this vast wealth has been how to get it to more populated regions where it can be used.

Source 3
Russia's northern location has continually held back development by restricting agricultural potential. Not only is most of the country not suitable for agriculture, but those regions that are arable can produce food for only part of the year.

Source 4
History has played an important part in Russian development. The Mongol conquest of the 13th century cut Russia off from the West just as the West was beginning an era of intellectual and technical development.

Source 5
Lack of access to the sea has long held back Russian development. Russia's seacoasts are poorly located in terms of enabling contact with other nations. They are either remote from markets or are frozen over for much of the year.

5. The difficulty Russia has had in transporting goods and people is discussed by sources
   - **A.** 1 and 3
   - **B.** 1, 2, and 5
   - **C.** 3 and 4
   - **D.** 4 and 5

6. That historical factors have had great influence on Russia's development is pointed out by source
   - **A.** 1
   - **B.** 2
   - **C.** 3
   - **D.** 4

CHALLENGER QUESTION

7. A problem of development that is not dealt with by any of the sources, but that has greatly influenced the Russian people is
   - **A.** ethnic diversity
   - **B.** foreign invasion
   - **C.** lack of precipitation
   - **D.** its cold climate

8. Taken together, all of the sources indicate that the economic and political development of Russia has been
   - **A.** relatively unhindered compared to that of other nations
   - **B.** faced with numerous geographical and historical obstacles
   - **C.** hindered only by the backwardness of its people
   - **D.** rapid during most of the 19th and 20th centuries

INDUSTRIALIZATION IN PRE-REVOLUTIONARY RUSSIA

Use the information below to answer questions 9 and 10.

Emancipation of the Serfs

Although the institution known as *serfdom* was banished in Russia, in actual fact, very little had changed for the Russian peasant. After their emancipation, the serfs were supposed to be completely free. However, this was not entirely the case. First of all, the peasants were required to pay for the land that they were given by the large landowners. Since most peasants had little money, these payments were stretched out over a 99-year period. This burden of mortgage payments to the large landowners left many peasants little better off than they had been before emancipation. In addition, much of the land received by the peasants was placed under the control of the *mir* or village, so that individual peasants had no land that they could really call their own.

9. Based on the information above, the situation for the Russian peasants had not changed following emancipation because the peasants
   - **A.** received little or no land
   - **B.** were still controlled by the landowners
   - **C.** were now required to pay taxes on their land
   - **D.** were required to pay for their land

10. Another problem for the peasants was that the land they received was
   - **A.** often scattered over a wide area
   - **B.** too small for them to make a living from
   - **C.** not under their direct control
   - **D.** used for purposes other than agriculture

GOVERNMENT PLANNING IN RUSSIA

Use the information below to answer questions 11 to 15.

Source 1
At the beginning of World War I, Russia had many brave soldiers, officers with military experience, and strong allies. What Russia lacked was industrial capacity. World War I was a war in which the ability to manufacture large amounts of weapons and supplies was more important than sheer numbers of brave soldiers.

Source 2
Russia suffered a series of military disasters during the first three years of World War I. Many of these disasters may be attributed to a shortage of equipment, but a large number were caused by the incompetence of the generals, who simply had no idea of how to fight a modern war.

Source 3
By the end of the first year of World War I, Russia was so short of military equipment that only one man in three had a rifle. Even those with rifles had only enough ammunition to fire a few rounds a day. Soldiers, armed only with bayonets, were launched against enemy positions. The resulting slaughter was to be expected.

Source 4
Russia was so poorly equipped for modern war that she was forced to divert all of her resources to the war effort. This resulted in severe shortages of food and other necessities. As a result, the urban poor could not afford to buy food. In the middle of winter, firewood was also unavailable. This led to considerable discontent.

Source 5
Russian leadership during the war must be blamed for many of the failures of the Russian army. The Czar and his government lacked the skills to conduct a modern war. In addition, under the influence of the evil monk Rasputin, the Czar's wife, Alexandra, undermined the authority of the Russian government.

11. According to the information above, at the beginning of World War I, Russia's most serious problem was

A. a shortage of manpower

B. inadequately trained soldiers

C. a lack of patriotism

D. inadequate industrial capacity

12. A major cause of Russia's many military disasters was

A. overconfident generals

B. the superior numbers of enemy soldiers

C. a shortage of military equipment

D. the severe winter weather

13. The war created a serious strain on Russia's civilian population. This was primarily because of

A. Russia's inability to fight a war and supply its civilian population with the necessities of life

B. the hoarding of foodstuffs and other goods by members of the upper classes

C. the blockade of Russia's western ports by the enemy

D. over-consumption of vital supplies by members of the military

CHALLENGER QUESTION

14. People began to lose faith in the Czar and his government because

A. the Czar was not considered an experienced military commander

B. Alexandra was secretly corresponding with the enemy

C. military failures together with the corrupting influence of Rasputin discredited the Czar

D. the Czar was blamed for Russia's lack of preparedness

15. The **most** significant result of the events/situation described in the sources was the

A. decision by the Czar to grant the Russian people some democratic privileges

B. fall of the Czar and the beginning of the Russian Revolution

C. surrender of Russia to Germany in 1917

D. loss to Germany of vast areas of Russian territory

Use the information below to answer questions 16 to 20.

Source 1
The son of a schoolteacher, this revolutionary leader was the intellectual and inspirational force behind the Bolshevik revolutionary movement. A good deal of his life was spent organizing his revolutionary movement from countries like Switzerland, as it was too dangerous for him to operate in Russia. At the beginning of the revolution, he was rushed back to Russia with the help of the Germans. Once there, he took over the revolutionary movement and brought communism to Russia.

Source 2
This brilliant writer has been termed "the father of communism." Born in Germany, he spent much of his life in exile. His two most important works *Das Kapital* (Capital) and *The Communist Manifesto* explained and popularized the philosophy of communism. Although he died before his dream of a communist revolution was realized, without his thought it is certain that modern communism would never have been created.

Source 3
This communist revolutionary began as a small time bandit in the Russian province of Georgia. Although he played only a small part in the 1917 Revolution, he gradually assumed greater and greater power as a part of the Communist Party. Eventually, he was able to eliminate his rivals and emerged as the undisputed leader of the new Soviet Union.

Source 4
An intellectual and revolutionary, he was one of the early leaders of the Bolshevik Party. After the overthrow of the czar, he emerged as the leader and organizer of the Red Army. His handling of military affairs was so successful that in an amazingly short time his new army was able to defeat all of his rivals and secure the place of communism in Russia.

CHALLENGER QUESTION

16. The revolutionary leader referred to in source 1 is

A. Joseph Stalin

B. Alexander Kerensky

C. Leon Trotsky

D. V.I. Lenin

CHALLENGER QUESTION

17. The philosopher referred to in source 2 is

A. V.I. Lenin

B. Karl Marx

C. Joseph Stalin

D. Leon Trotsky

CHALLENGER QUESTION

18. The revolutionary referred to in source 3 is

A. V.I. Lenin

B. Karl Marx

C. Joseph Stalin

D. Leon Trotsky

CHALLENGER QUESTION

19. The revolutionary referred to in source 4 is

A. V.I. Lenin

B. Karl Marx

C. Joseph Stalin

D. Leon Trotsky

CHALLENGER QUESTION

20. The one person whose dynamism and energy is most responsible for the success of the 1917 revolution in Russia is described in source

A. 1

B. 2

C. 3

D. 4

21. In 1921, it was decided that the economy of the Soviet Union needed a boost. As a result, the New Economic Policy was introduced. This policy was

A. a complete return to the economic system of Czarist Russia

B. the implementation of long term planning of all aspects of the Soviet economy

C. a partial return to capitalism in order to jump-start the economy

D. to collectivize all agriculture in Russia

Use the information below to answer questions 22 to 26.

Results of the First Five-Year Plan

Source 1
The First Five-Year Plan achieved dramatic results. Between 1928 and 1933, industrial output increased enormously. The number of industrial workers increased from three million to six million. Oil production doubled. Electrical power increased by 550% and machinery production increased by 400%. The number of workers on cooperative farms increased from less than two percent to over 60%. So successful was the First Five-Year Plan that it was pronounced complete before the end of the fifth year.

Source 2
The enormous increase in industrial power created by the First Five-Year Plan was achieved only through the hard work and sacrifice of the Soviet population. Workers were frequently overworked and forced to meet rigorous production quotas. Those workers who did not keep up with the pace of the factory were often brutally punished, and factory managers who failed to achieve assigned goals were often imprisoned or even executed.

Source 3
During the First Five-Year Plan, working conditions were often dangerous or unhealthy. Safety standards were ignored and workers were bombarded with propaganda aimed at getting them to work harder. As a result, injuries and deaths from job related accidents were very high.

Source 4
The goals of the First Five-Year Plan were achieved at high cost. Slave labour was used on some projects, especially those in Siberia and the northern U.S.S.R. Tens of thousands of political prisoners laboured under harsh conditions constructing dams, canals, and roads. Thousands of overworked and underpaid slave labourers were literally worked to death.

Source 5
The First Five-Year Plan was least successful in agriculture. Collectivization was met with strong resistance and the government responded by using brutal force to get the farmers to comply. Farmers were evicted from their lands, and their crops and livestock were confiscated. Peasants responded by often destroying their own farm buildings and produce. As a result, there was a horrific famine. It is estimated that up to 14 million peasants died in the government-induced famine; one of the greatest acts of brutality in world history.

22. The over-all theme of the sources is that

A. the First Five-Year Plan was spectacularly successful

B. attempts to industrialize the U.S.S.R. failed dismally

C. industrialization in the U.S.S.R. was achieved at great cost

D. brutality was common under the government of Joseph Stalin

23. Attempts to modernize Soviet industry were least successful in the area of

A. agriculture

B. transportation

C. mining

D. energy

24. A supporter of central planning would justify the hardship and brutality of industrialization by pointing out that

A. the creation of a worker's paradise required some sacrifice

B. the workers were exploited during the early Industrial Revolution

C. industrialization is not possible without some hardship

D. those persons harmed by industrialization were enemies of the state

25. A supporter of central planning would **most likely** proclaim communism's superiority by pointing out

A. the successes of the First Five-Year Plan in agriculture

B. that most soviet citizens cheerfully endured the hardships necessary for industrialization

C. the spectacular achievements indicated by source 1

D. that goals in all areas of economic development were reached or exceeded

CHALLENGER QUESTION

26. The paradox or contradiction illustrated by the successes of the First Five-Year Plan is that

A. only members of the government shared in its successes

B. it only succeeded because of the dedication of the Soviet people

C. success was due to the sacrifices of the people it was supposed to help

D. the Soviet Union relied heavily on its natural resources for its industrial success

27. The process of changing the Soviet Union into a complete totalitarian state during the 1930s was known as

A. Stalinization

B. Authoritarianism

C. Absolutism

D. Despotism

Use the information below to answer questions 28 and 29.

The Great Purges

Source 1
Stalin's decision to eliminate hundreds of thousands of his own countrymen during the 1930s served a simple purpose. He created a country where he alone was dominant. All rivals were eliminated and all other Soviet citizens reduced to a state of subservience.

Source 2
During the 1930s, Stalin embarked on a policy of eliminating all of his enemies, both real and imagined. Stalin's mental state was an important factor in this event. Stalin trusted no one and feared almost everyone. As a result, the number of victims he required in order to feel safe was truly enormous.

Source 3
Stalin's elimination of millions of Soviet citizens during the 1930s had a disastrous effect on the Soviet Union. The Soviet Union became a place of terror where no one knew whom to trust and where a simple word could lead to charges of treason.

Source 4
The number of Stalin's victims rose into the millions. Many of the brightest and the best were killed, including 90% of the senior officers of the Red Army. The result was a terrible loss for the Soviet Union. In addition, the country was terribly unprepared for the coming war with Germany.

28. According to the sources, Stalin's motive for the elimination of so many of his own people was

A. to eliminate enemies of communism

B. to reduce the nation to a state of terror

C. both political and psychological

D. fear of assassination

29. The purges impacted the Soviet

A. economy

B. political system

C. political system, the Soviet psyche, and the Soviet military

D. culture and the Soviet economy

THE CENTRAL ECONOMY

Use the information below to answer questions 30 to 34.

All economic systems attempt to answer five basic economic questions:

1. What goods and services should be produced?
2. How goods and services should be produced?
3. For whom the goods and services should be produced?
4. How much should be produced?
5. How fast should the economy grow?

30. Before determining the answer to question 1 in a centrally planned economy, it must be determined what goods and services

A. are most needed

B. are most desired

C. can be best afforded

D. provide the greatest profits

31. In a centrally planned economy, when determining the answer to question 2, it must also be determined which method of production would

A. have the least environmental impact

B. produce the most goods for the least cost

C. provide the greatest benefits to society as a whole

D. produce the product most quickly

32. When attempting to answer question 3 in a centrally planned economy, a key question to ask is "What members of society

A. most need what is produced?"

B. can best afford what is produced?"

C. are least able to afford what is produced?"

D. are most deserving of what is produced?"

33. When determining the answer to question 4 in a centrally planned economy, the **most** important factor would be

A. what is the demand for the product

B. how much of the product competitors are producing

C. what is the availability of resources

D. how much does society need the product

34. When determining the answer to question 5 in a centrally planned economy, the **most** important factor would be

A. the rise and fall of the business cycle

B. world demand for goods and services

C. decisions made by government economic planners

D. the availability and price of raw materials

35. In attempting to determine what goods should be produced in the Soviet Union, a factor that had little influence on the final decision was

A. availability of raw materials

B. military considerations

C. consumer demand

D. demand for labour

36. In much of the Soviet Union, most types of consumer goods were available from only one source and variety was extremely limited. The principle of the market economy that the Soviet command economy was ignoring was that of

A. individualism

B. competition

C. private property

D. state intervention

37. The principle on which a centrally planned economy is based is that of

A. national growth

B. individual freedom

C. personal gain

D. collective good

Use the following information to answer questions 38 to 42.

Disadvantages of Central Planning

1. Individual initiative is discouraged.
2. Huge government bureaucracies are needed.
3. Individual freedom is restricted.
4. Consumer demands are often ignored.
5. Economic goals are often not met due to the complexity of central planning.

38. A problem of central planning in the Soviet Union was that most workers seldom did anything without being told. This attitude is reflected by disadvantage

A. 1

B. 2

C. 3

D. 4

39. An historic characteristic of Soviet society has been a shortage of everyday items such as flashlight batteries, toiletries, and other household items. This characteristic is a result of disadvantage

A. 2

B. 3

C. 4

D. 5

CHALLENGER QUESTION

40. During the 1970s, a Soviet textile plant applied to change the colour of one of its fabrics from blue to red. A planning committee had to study the impact of the proposed change and took several months to approve the application. The disadvantage of central planning that **best** reflects this is disadvantage

A. 2

B. 3

C. 4

D. 5

41. Central planning that provides facilities for the benefit of the entire population illustrates the positive aspects of disadvantage

A. 1

B. 2

C. 3

D. 4

42. As the Soviet economy evolved, it became more and more difficult for it to achieve its economic goals. By the 1980s, production goals were constantly being missed, especially in the areas of consumer goods and agriculture. As a result, it became obvious to many Soviet officials that major reforms were needed to correct the system. The situation is reflected by disadvantage

A. 2

B. 3

C. 4

D. 5

Use the information below to answer questions 43 to 47.

Source 1

The dressing room of the Edmonton Oilers
Brad: *Sergei, how are you and your wife adjusting to life in Canada?*

Sergei: *Pretty well, but we still have a few things to get used to.*
Brad: *Such as?*

Sergei: *Well, the other day my wife went grocery shopping for the first time. She came home with about 100 kg of meat. There was no room in the fridge for anything else.*
Brad: *Why did she do that?*

Sergei: *She was afraid that the next time she went shopping the store would be out of meat.*

Source 2

Pavel stopped his small car in front of the block of apartments where he lived. After carefully locking the car, he removed the side mirror and the windshield wipers. He took them into the apartment with him. Tomorrow he will reinstall them.

Source 3

News Item
Today in a Moscow courtroom, 21 year old Nicolai Strelnichov was sentenced to 10 years in a labour camp. The judge handed down this lenient sentence on account of the age of the accused. The judge cautioned Strelnichov to use his prison time to reform. Hoarding of goods was a serious and selfish crime. It not only contributed to the illegal sale of these goods at high prices, but also deprived ordinary citizens of their use.

Source 4

"Sasa, what is that noise?"
"American music mother. A band called the Doors."
"It is a terrible sound. Where did you get it?"
"On the Black Market. It cost me 200 rubles."
"200 rubles! Are you crazy? That is a terrible price and it's against the law to shop on the Black market. "
"Mother, even police officers shop on the market. Even you have shopped there."
"Only for important things. And I never spent 200 rubles for anything."

43. All of the sources reflect the problem of

A. supply and demand in a market economy

B. self-sufficiency in a traditional economy

C. shortages in a centrally planned economy

D. sale of contraband in a market economy

CHALLENGER QUESTION

44. The cultural confusion described in source 1 occurred because of

A. a belief in the superiority of the mixed economy

B. a lack of understanding concerning the workings of a market economy

C. confusion over the law of supply and demand

D. confusion over the value of the Canadian dollar

45. The source that showed that the law of supply and demand functions even in a centrally planned economy is

A. source 1

B. source 2

C. source 3

D. source 4

CHALLENGER QUESTION

46. In source 2, Pavel's actions were prompted by

A. concern that the products might malfunction

B. a desire to understand how the items work

C. concern over vandalism

D. fear of theft of goods in short supply

47. The fact that there has traditionally been a chronic shortage of goods in the Soviet Union is depicted by sources

A. 1 and 2

B. 2 and 3

C. 3 and 4

D. 1 and 3

Use the information below to answer questions 48 to 53.

Source 1
Central planning has proven to be a hopeless failure. In the Soviet Union, economic goals were constantly missed. Its population was doomed to live a life of eternal poverty. As a result, the more talented Soviet citizens escaped from the country whenever they could.

Source 2
Shortages, poor service, and goods of inferior quality were the norm in the U.S.S.R. This was entirely due to the weaknesses of central planning. It is simply not possible to plan every single aspect of a modern economy.

Source 3
The concept of central planning has been unfairly condemned. In fact, central planning in the Soviet Union achieved many of its goals. There was no unemployment or poverty. Citizens had access to free medical care and low cost housing. Everyone received enough to eat and basic pleasures were affordable to the average citizen.

Source 4
Those persons who condemn central planning do so in ignorance. Governments in all societies use central planning. The building of national highways, the construction of schools and hospitals, and the building of public facilities such as libraries and swimming pools are all examples of central planning. Not even the strongly capitalist United States leaves all of these programs up to the private sector.

Source 5
World War II was a classic example of the value of central planning. All of the major combatants, including Canada, the United States, and Britain exercised strict control over their economies during the war. Scarce goods were rationed, businesses were told what to produce, and production of luxury goods was reduced to a minimum. Without such strict control of the economy the war could not have been won by the allies.

48. The various sources are in disagreement over

A. the benefits of central planning

B. whether or not the government should offer services

C. the difficulty of administering a centrally planned economy

D. the success of central planning in a market economy

49. Central planning has been shown to be of value in times of emergency, as illustrated by source

A. 1

B. 3

C. 4

D. 5

50. A problem of Soviet society was the defection of many of its most talented citizens to countries where they could profit more from their abilities. As a result, hockey players, ballet stars, and other skilled athletes often sought political asylum in non-communist countries such as the United States. This fact is referred to in source

A. 1

B. 2

C. 3

D. 5

51. That central planning in the Soviet Union was not a failure, attested to by the fact that it achieved many of its goals, is maintained in source

A. 2

B. 3

C. 4

D. 5

52. The opinion that modern economies are simply too complex to leave to central planning is reflected in source

A. 2

B. 3

C. 4

D. 5

53. Central planning is useful when governments attempt to provide facilities that are intended to benefit the entire population, as indicated by source

A. 1

B. 2

C. 3

D. 4

Use the information below to answer questions 54 and 55.

Full Employment in the Soviet Union

In the Soviet Union, all citizens were guaranteed employment. One of the benefits of this practice was that the state did not have to support those workers who lost their jobs. The obvious benefit for the workers was that they did not have to fear any downturns in the economy. A job for life meant that the average Soviet citizen lived in complete security.

There was, however, a price to be paid for full employment. Workers often took advantage of the fact that they could not be fired and thus performed substandard work. Absenteeism was also very high, especially on Fridays and Mondays. In addition, the promise of full employment often meant that several workers were hired to do the job of one person. This encouraged workers to be idle and do as little as possible in order to make the jobs last. As a result, Soviet productivity was low and the quality of their goods was poor.

54. As practiced in the Soviet Union, the policy of full employment was implemented in order to

A. save the government money

B. illustrate the superiority of central planning

C. provide its citizens with economic security

D. furnish industry with a reliable workforce

CHALLENGER QUESTION

55. A supporter of the market economy would point out that the low productivity, caused as a result of the U.S.S.R.'s full employment policy, was due to the

A. low level of training of Soviet workers

B. complexity of the planned economy

C. lack of faith of workers in the Soviet system

D. Soviet workers having little incentive to perform well

Use the information below to answer questions 56 and 57.

Hoarding in the Soviet Union

One of the characteristics of the Soviet system was a chronic shortage of consumer goods. As a result, consumers engaged in illegal activities such as hoarding. Anxious shoppers bought up any product that might not be readily available. This, of course, resulted in a shortage of the product for any other shoppers that had missed the product on the day that it was in stock. Despite severe penalties for the hoarding of goods, the practice was commonplace. Anyone with a surplus of a particular product could use his private stock to trade for other items in short supply or even sell the private stock at inflated prices.

56. The problem of hoarding in the Soviet Union was caused by the fact that in a centrally planned economy

A. wages were deliberately kept low

B. products were often shoddily made

C. basic needs were often disregarded

D. consumer demand was usually ignored

57. The principle of socialism the Soviet Union attempted to uphold by making the practice of hoarding illegal was that of

A. job security

B. equal opportunity

C. opposition to private property

D. public ownership of the means of production

Use the information below to answer questions 58 and 59.

Public Transport in the U.S.S.R.

In the Soviet Union, certain services were provided at a very low price. The price of a ride on the Moscow subway was only about seven cents and has been that price for several decades. Similarly, bus service was also cheap and readily available.

58. In the Soviet centrally planned economy, the market economy principle of

A. profit motive does not exist

B. supply and demand does not exist

C. competition does not exist

D. private ownership does not exist

59. A supporter of a command economy would justify the subsidization of public transport by pointing out that

A. inflation in the Soviet Union was quite low

B. the low cost transport was proof of the superiority of the Soviet system

C. the low wages in the Soviet Union meant the average citizen could not afford expensive transport

D. in a modern command economy, low cost transport was a necessity

Use the information below to answer question 60.

Ownership of Consumer Items for Selected Countries in 1984

Country	Persons per Telephone	Persons per Television	Persons per Automobile
Canada	2	3	3
Britain	2	3	3
France	3	3	3
Brazil	20	12	15
Soviet Union	2	14	40

CHALLENGER QUESTION

60. A comparison of the statistics would seem to indicate that

A. levels of consumer goods in the U.S.S.R. were more similar to that of a developing nation like Brazil than other nations

B. economic priorities in market economies focussed on capital goods

C. the Soviet Union lacked the resources to produce large numbers of consumer goods

D. technical skills in the Soviet Union trailed those of most developed nations

Use the information below to answer question 61.

Selected Data for Various Countries – 1984				
Country	**Persons per Physician**	**Infant Mortality (per 1000)**	**Literacy Rate**	**Military Spending (% of GNP)**
Canada	560	12	99	1.80
Britain	770	14	99	5.25
France	625	10	99	4.62
United States	565	12	99	5.98
Soviet Union	289	28	99	12.66

61. According to the data, the country that was most concerned with national security was

A. Canada

B. Britain

C. the United States

D. the Soviet Union

QUALITY OF LIFE

Use the information below to answer questions 62 to 66.

Source 1
Life under central planning may be described as dreary and restrictive. The standard of living in the Soviet Union was quite low by Canadian or American standards. The quality and variety of goods and services was extremely limited. People lived dull lives with very little prospect of change. Citizens did not even have the right to move about their own country freely, but rather, were required to carry identification cards that listed their assigned place of residence.

Source 2
Central planning in the Soviet Union was very successful. Imagine a society in which there was no poverty; people had guaranteed jobs; health care and education were free; and the basic needs of everyday life were provided at low cost.

Source 3
Try to picture what it might be like to live in a centrally planned economy. There is no such thing as private property, therefore, people are not free to start up their own businesses, own land for farming, or even leave their homes to their heirs. The state controlled everything. People were not allowed to do anything for themselves, and as a result, all citizens were doomed to a life of mediocrity.

Source 4
Life for the worker under central planning was a kind of Utopia. There were no harsh bosses constantly threatening the workers with instant dismissal. Workers were paid fairly and received many social benefits. There was no upper or lower class, no rich and no poor. All people were treated equally and there was mutual respect for everyone.

Source 5
The supposed equality of central planning was a joke. Senior members of the Soviet Communist Party, top athletes, and important scientists, received special rights and privileges. There were even special stores where only the privileged few could shop. In addition, this elite group had access to better housing, could travel more freely, and could more easily obtain scarce goods. As a result, the supposedly classless planned economy had an all too obvious upper class that strove to maintain its dominant position within Soviet society.

62. The various sources are in disagreement over the issue of whether or not central planning

A. is necessary in a mixed economy

B. was fair to workers

C. was successful in achieving its goals

D. provided opportunity for advancement

63. The importance of equality is emphasized in source

A. 1

B. 2

C. 3

D. 4

CHALLENGER QUESTION

64. The restrictions on personal freedom that existed in a centrally planned economy are outlined in sources

A. 1 and 3

B. 2 and 4

C. 4 and 5

D. 1 and 5

65. That real equality did not exist in the Soviet Union is suggested in source

A. 2

B. 3

C. 4

D. 5

66. The security provided by a centrally planned economy is emphasized in source

A. 1

B. 2

C. 4

D. 5

NOTES

Economic Growth: Canada

ECONOMIC GROWTH: CANADA

Table of Correlations

Topic	Concepts	Related Concepts, Terms, and Facts	Related Questions
HOW TECHNOLOGY HAS AFFECTED AND CONTINUES TO AFFECT OUR WAY OF LIFE	Technological change	Utilization of technology Primary industry Secondary industry Tertiary industry Innovation Robotics Computers The Information Revolution The social, economic, political, environmental, and cultural impact of technological change	1 – 19
THE MIXED ECONOMY	In a mixed economy, how are economic decisions made by both public and private sectors?	Labour-management relations The importance of the public sector	20 – 42
QUALITY OF LIFE	How is quality of life influenced by the beliefs and values of a mixed economy? How is the quality of life influenced by technological change?	How lifestyles in a mixed economy are different from those in a pure market or pure centrally planned economy Lifestyles resulting from a mixed economy The social, economic, spiritual, and physical impact of the mixed economy	43 – 58

TECHNOLOGY

Technology has affected our way of life and continues to influence our future. Students will need to make decisions about how we should respond to technological change, how it affects the way people work, and how it is affecting our way of life. Economic growth and technological change go together and affect the quality of life in numerous ways.

Utilization

Utilization is an abstract term that involves how we use things in the world. In this curriculum context it is associated with the terms primary, secondary, tertiary, and quaternary industries.

Primary Industries

Primary industries are those industries that obtain natural resources and raw materials from the Earth including the sea. It is helpful to think of them as **extractive activities**. Examples include those industries where minerals are taken out of the ground such as coal, oil, uranium, and iron ore. Fishing is sometimes regarded as a primary industry where fish are caught and taken from the ocean. Harvesting of trees in the lumber industry is also considered as a primary source of raw material. Students need to be able to differentiate between the various orders of industry and understand the distinctions between primary, secondary, tertiary, and quaternary industries.

Secondary Industries

Secondary industries are those that involve taking natural resources and raw materials and turning them or processing them into finished or semi-finished goods. It is helpful to think of them as **manufacturing activities**. Examples are, the manufacturing of iron and steel for car parts, the manufacturing of cotton products into clothes, and the smelting of steel to produce sheet metal.

An oil refinery is considered as secondary industry where crude oil or tar sands from a primary source is turned into gasoline and other oil products. The manufacture of plastics, which is a by-product of the petro-chemical industry, is also an example of a secondary industry.

Other examples include a fish-processing plant where raw fish is processed and packaged for distribution; and a lumber mill where raw materials such as softwood lumber is turned into boards, planks, and other manufactured products.

Tertiary Industries

Tertiary industries can be considered as the range of service industries such as banking, teaching, and running a store in a shopping mall. The selling of merchandise that has been produced by a secondary industry is considered as an activity associated with tertiary industry.

Quaternary Industries

More recently, the term "quaternary industries" has emerged which describes many of the activities associated with the information age society. It includes companies that are involved in gathering data, data processing, information processing, and business intelligence. The distinction between tertiary and quaternary industries is a little fuzzy but a general rule would be that quaternary industries are associated with information dissemination.

Innovations and Robotics

Innovations and robotics have gone hand in hand with automation, specialization, and mass production. Innovation is essentially the act of introducing something new. An invention, on the other hand, is a term that is very similar but implies a discovery or the use of a new device.

Examples of innovations are introducing a new invention to society, a new method of production, a new system of thinking, and a new set of management techniques. Examples of some major innovations throughout history are the application of the wheel, the development of the internal combustion engine, different ways of using computers, and products associated with digital technologies. Students can think of which innovations have had the most impact in society. One classic example used in many textbooks is Henry Ford's production line and the production of the Model T-Ford.

Robotics involves the science or study of the technology associated with the design and application of robots. Robots are used in many industries today and although they have "space age" associations, they are used in everything from car manufacture to bomb disposal. Japan may still be considered "the world leader" when it comes to innovations associated with robotics. Many military industrial complexes are also investigating and applying the use of robotics for defence and warfare possibilities and applications.

Cybernation is a modern trend that refers to the use of computers to control and supervise other machines. Many science fiction stories and movies are based on plots where machines take over control from human beings and lead to potential world or territorial domination. Such is the case in the recent film "I, Robot" from the 1960's book by Isaac Azimov. However, cybernation or machine monitoring and supervision is used increasingly for tasks from launching the space shuttle to heart monitors in hospitals.

Implications for Society

Innovations, robotics and cybernation raise questions for society about values. People also hold different attitudes towards these trends. Some feel it is "good thing" while others believe it is "not a good thing." There is a range of views involving a scale, continuum or spectrum on issues associated with this topic.

In the provincial achievement test, students are given scenarios, sources, and viewpoints that reflect differing opinions about these trends. It is important for students to understand the different viewpoints being proposed, and to analyse the negative and positive (or indifferent) positions taken. From these viewpoints, or sources, students are asked to infer a position, or understand a common theme in the source material. There may be a prediction in the source material, in which case students need to weigh the options. In addition, students may be asked to evaluate an alternative position from that presented by the source material. Ultimately, these questions involve making judgements about the implications for the "good" of society. **Careful reading of the source material or viewpoints is essential.** Students should not be afraid to underline or annotate (write notes) on their achievement test booklets to clarify the positions in the source material.

Some common areas include:

- the response of workers to machines
- workers' rights and machines
- technological change and unemployment
- advances in technology are not clearly understood
- resistance to change in society is a way of life
- resistance to technological change is largely ineffective

MIXED ECONOMY

The notion of a mixed economy is an outdated concept because most economies in the world today are mixed. Most nations have economies that involve a degree of intervention by government and free market enterprise, even in "communist" countries such as Cuba, and North Korea. Countries such as those that are members of the G7 or G8 with Russia, are also mixed economies where there is some government control as well as free enterprise.

At the time the original Program of Studies for Grade 9 was developed, Canada was seen as a country that represented the "middle ground" between the capitalistic free enterprise image of the USA and the communist, state-directed image of the former USSR.

In general, the notion of the mixed economy is that decisions are made in both the public and private sectors to benefit the economy. However, as stated it would be difficult to find a nation today where this is not the case.

Scarcity

The concept of scarcity is one of the basic ideas in economics. It is tied to the notion that all goods and services are limited. For example, the more demand there is for a product the less there will be, unless the supply for that product is increased. Because there are limits on most resources, choices must be made in regard to that resource. The price of a product is also reflected by its scarcity and in general this is related to its quantity on the earth and the demand for it. In a mixed economy where the private sector and government coexist, the market will reflect decisions made in both sectors.

In Canada, oil and natural gas are limited or finite resources as they are elsewhere in the world. If the world demand for oil or gas goes up, then production will increase worldwide. This may be seen as a benefit to Canada and particularly Alberta because the price for buying the product goes up. As a consequence, it is likely that oil and gas will be extracted more rapidly (increase in supply), and/or new reserves will be found and tapped. On the other hand, the result of an increased demand may mean that the cost of gasoline "at the pumps" goes up affecting "consumers' wallets" and the cost of heating houses with gas in Canada also rises. The rise in prices leads to inflation.

Sometimes, because of the rapid rise in prices for commodities such as oil and gas it is necessary for the government to take action and to protect the consumer. This is called **regulation**. When the government does this, it is said to be **intervening** in the market place and affecting the price through policy decisions. An illustration of this is the decision by the Provincial Government of Alberta to subsidize the price of a natural gas to the consumer when it goes over a certain market price. Some economists regard this as manipulation of the marketplace by artificial means.

On the other hand, if the world supply of oil becomes plentiful rather than scarce, there is a tendency for the price of oil to drop in a free-market situation. At a certain point it may be necessary for the government to intervene and artificially control the price. In the past countries in the Middle East have manipulated the market by controlling supply and demand of oil for political reasons. This has led to the development of a world economic organization called OPEC (Oil Petroleum Exporting Countries). This body decides how much oil should be produced and exported by various member countries. Also OPEC helps to decide the world price for oil by common agreement by its members.

Oil and natural gas exploration and development takes place only where it is profitable or perceived as profitable. Largely this is due to increased demand for these products. This has lead to the phenomenal growth in the energy sector during the past few years. As a result, places like Fort McMurray have experienced rapid growth and industrialization. New oil plants have been built, or expanded and further plants are being planned in response to the demand for oil and gas as products.

Conversely, if the oil or gas reserves in Canada become severely depleted or dry up, then it is more than likely that the industry will go into economic decline because of the **scarcity** of the resources. All projections do not support this at present but the quantity of these products is finite and they are considered as non-renewable resources. In the past "booming towns" became "ghost towns" after the resources were extracted. Famous examples of ghost towns include the towns that sprang up during the Klondike Gold Rush; the same is true for some coal mining towns when coal mining no longer became profitable.

For the economic growth and quality of life questions, students may have to decide whether or not such developments improve the quality of life and who benefits. Students may be asked to decide whether such developments create a dangerous dependency on one particular resource and its implications. They may also have to consider tradeoffs between development and the environment.

Factors of Production

Traditionally, factors of production are seen as land, labour, and capital. That is physical space, a workforce and money and investment. Associated with the factors are four main economic questions:

- What goods and services should be produced?
- How should goods and services be produced?
- How should goods and services be distributed?
- Who decides on the allocation of these resources, methods of production and the distribution of goods?

The last question is very important because in a 'free' market economy, the natural conditions of the market place control these factors with business people and investors risking their capital. By contrast, the mixed or command economy exists, where factors of production are controlled by significant government decisions and government intervention. There is often a fine line between influence and interference.

Role of Business, Labour, Government, and Consumers

In a mixed economy, businesses are encouraged to grow through a combination of the market place and government involvement.

In a mixed economy, **the role of business** is essentially to take risks and to make a profit from products and services while at the same time providing employment for citizens. Businesses look for "good" places to locate that will be cost effective, efficient and profitable for the production of their products.

The location of a business depends upon a number of factors including access to markets, availability of raw materials, transport costs, energy costs and availability of a work force. Government can encourage businesses to locate in a certain area using certain levers. By providing tax breaks, subsidies and promoting the benefits of living in a certain community, government representatives can encourage entrepreneurs to make decisions to set up their businesses in locations across Canada, in Alberta or in a municipality. Governments at all three levels (federal, provincial, municipal) can exert considerable influence in the decision-making process.

The role of labour is a significant factor in the mixed economy. A labour force is necessary to run industries or businesses. Some industries are said to be labour intensive. These industries require large numbers of people to work in factories or plants. Other industries are not so labour intensive and require just a few people to operate the businesses. The wages that workers make is often a large expenditure in a company budget and these wages can reflect the profitability of the company. When times are good and company profits are high, wages can be increased and vice-versa. This will depend upon the owners of the company. In some companies, a few key people, or the owners decide the questions associated with the factors of production. In other companies, the workers can take on a major role in deciding these questions. The former case is sometimes referred to as a "top down" system, the latter is described as a "horizontal organization."

Usually, companies make decisions involving wages independently of government in a mixed economy. However, if the employees do not regard the wages as fair, the government may have to step in and decide what is regarded as an appropriate wage for workers. Also in a mixed economy the government may legislate (or make laws) about a minimum wage which is the lowest amount of money that can be paid to an employee for a unit (an hour) of work.

Government can help by giving tax breaks or subsidies to certain industries. For example, if the government wants to encourage technology related business to come to a certain area, they may offer land for development at a certain price or reduce business taxes. Governments can also guarantee business with certain contracts. For example, a government may guarantee that they will purchase fifteen jets or ten helicopters built by a certain manufacturer. The government is responsible for setting regulations and laws.

Consumers affect the marketplace by "dollar voting", and influence supply and demand through their decisions and hence the price of the product. Consumers buy products that they like from their limited resources such as their wages or savings (or credit). In turn, this stimulates the marketplace and more goods are produced. The company profits, as do the workers (depending upon agreements), and the shareholders. For example, the iPod has been an extremely profitable product for Apple Computers in Canada and the world, and has turned the company around in the computer marketplace largely dominated by such companies as Microsoft, IBM and Dell.

Labour Management Relations

Working conditions and wages are very important to all people. Basically, a worker wants to get the best working conditions possible and the most amount of money in return for his or her work. An employer, on the other hand, may want to provide just the “basic” working conditions and the minimum amount of wages to a worker in return for his or her work.

The process of labour management relations is to address what are fair working conditions and wages. The employer and employee do this through various means, often through "collective bargaining" or negotiation. In some cases, management is represented by a group of people from the upper levels of the company (such as the president, vice-president, a shareholder representative, etc.) and associations or unions represent the employees. The two sides try to negotiate conditions and wages "at the table" where both groups try to agree on conditions of employment.

Under most circumstances this can be done peacefully and effectively such as recent cases involving Ford, and GM Canada. Under other circumstances, conflict arises involving walkouts, demonstrations, and strikes such as the recent strike by teachers in British Columbia and the labour dispute at a meat processing plant in Brooks, Alberta.

Governments at the federal and provincial levels set labour laws in Canada. Much that happens in the Province of Alberta is generally governed by provincial labour legislation. Some groups deemed "essential services" are not allowed to strike. Examples are people employed in the emergency services such as police, fire fighters and ambulance workers. It is a condition of their contracts that they are not able to strike.

In some difficult cases where there is conflict between labour and management, the government can take action. They can appoint a mediator to resolve a dispute between two sides, and they can legislate groups back to work if they are on strike.

Public and Private Sectors

The public sector is the area of the economy that is owned wholly by the people or the government of Canada whereas the private sector is the area where private entrepreneurs or groups of business people own businesses. Both the government and private sector provide goods and services.

The public sector is a large sector in the Canadian economy. It includes all government departments, services, and offices. Examples include all government departments such as Revenue Canada that deals with taxation, and Parks Canada that deals with national parks. The RCMP, which is responsible for law enforcement, and Canada's military forces are part of the public sector. Other examples include Canada Post, and the Canadian Mint, which are owned by the people of Canada. However, some postal outlets are privately operated like those that are to be found in some retail outlets.

In the past the Government of Canada has also owned and operated "business enterprises" which have competed with the private sector such as Petro-Canada, Canadian National Railways, and Air Canada. Today, most of these companies have been sold to the private sector largely as a result of a change in political philosophy that believes that the government should stay out of the market place and not own "companies". It has also been argued that these companies were given certain economic advantages over private business because they were government owned. A valuable source of information is to be found in *The Canadian Encyclopedia* at http://www.thecanadianencyclopedia.com/

Businesses that are wholly owned and operated by federal or provincial organizations are usually referred to as Crown Corporations, whereas land that is owned and operated by these levels of government is known as Crown Land. According to *The Canadian Encyclopedia 2000*, less than 11% of Canada's land was privately owned, 41% was federal and 48% was provincial Crown Land.

Beliefs and values

The values underlying Canada's mixed economy are that we support social equality, that we are a compassionate society, that we help people in emergency situations, and that we value "universality". It is for these reasons that Canada has adopted a social safety net for all where social security benefits are provided to the less fortunate, Unemployment Benefit is given to the unemployed, and senior citizens receive a pension under the Canada Pension Plan. Child Tax Credits are also given to help families with limited or low incomes.

As Canadians, we also believe in the fairness of a policy of graduated taxation where the more you earn the more you pay. Although this results in relatively high taxation, it also supports the cost of running the various social programs. Health care (or Medicare), education and social services are **provided to all** based on the belief of **universal access** and not based on an individual's ability to pay for these services.

These social and societal values are extremely important in differentiating Canada from some other countries of the world including the USA.

QUALITY OF LIFE

The quality of life is both an abstract and real term that involves the opportunities that individuals in society have to enjoy lifestyles. It is connected to spiritual, mental, and physical aspects of life as well as social and economic, factors. External and internal conditions and perceptions determine the quality of life. It is also a relative term, and for many, a judgement about the state of well-being.

In a mixed economy the combination of private ownership and public involvement in the economy produces a quality of life where the individual is not completely alone. The system is a balance between private and public ownership whereby citizens do not have to be completely self-sufficient. The state does provide social and economic support for the disadvantaged or those that have become unemployed. In contrast to the American model, where there is more emphasis on self-sufficiency and the ability to pay for services such as health care, the mixed economy provides a happy medium between completely private and completely state run enterprises.

ECONOMIC GROWTH: CANADA

HOW TECHNOLOGICAL CHANGES HAVE AFFECTED OUR WAY OF LIFE

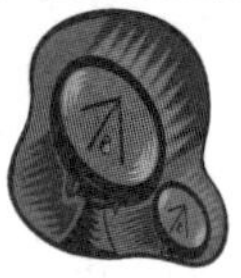

Use the information below to answer questions 1 to 3.

Source 1

As far as the eye could see, the surface of the ground was studded with derricks, and from each, like the silver webs of some gigantic spider, there sprang the steel pipes that carried the most important industrial product of the 20th century: oil.

Source 2

The inside of the giant mill seemed like Hell on Earth. Streams of molten metal poured from giant furnaces. Great hammers pounded the white hot metal. The air was filled with an immense roar, punctuated with the sharper sounds of great machines. Steel: it is one of the basic building materials of the 20th century.

Source 3

The sharp cries of sea birds filled the air. Gulls swept around the net looking for any opportunity to join in the harvest of the sea. On deck the fishermen attended to the job of pulling in the heavy net, ignoring the keening birds.

Source 4

As the teachers watched, the great orange buses pulled up in front of the school, disgorging their human cargo. The start of another school year! So many energetic young minds to stimulate and influence.

Source 5

Nine o'clock! The clerk turned the sign on the door to read "Open" and unlocked the door. Within a few minutes the first potential customer was walking the aisles, perusing the merchandise. Perhaps this would be another good day.

1. Primary industries are depicted in sources

A. 1 and 2

B. 1 and 3

C. 2 and 4

D. 4 and 5

2. A secondary industry is depicted in source

A. 1 **B.** 2

C. 3 **D.** 4

3. Tertiary industries are depicted in sources

A. 1 and 2

B. 2 and 3

C. 3 and 4

D. 4 and 5

Use the information below to answer questions 4 to 7.

Reaction to Technological Change

Scenario 1

During the 18th and 19th centuries, groups of textile workers, such as spinners and weavers, broke into the newly constructed textile factories and destroyed textile machinery. They hoped that through their actions, they could halt the change to mechanization that was robbing them of their livelihood.

Scenario 2

Factory workers in the 19th century, angry at their appalling working conditions, low pay, and continued push towards mechanization, would sometimes remove their wooden shoes and toss them into the gear mechanisms of the textile machines. This caused the gears to jam and sometimes break. Since the wooden shoes were called clogs, this led to the phrase "to clog up the works." In Belgium and France, where the same wooden shoes were called "sabots," such actions were referred to as sabotage.

Scenario 3

In the 1960s and 1970s, banks and department stores mailed computer punch cards along with customers' bills. Some customers would deliberately punch extra holes in the cards in order to force those businesses to use human workers to process their accounts instead of machines.

Scenario 4

At the beginning of the automobile age, motor-powered vehicles were extremely unreliable. The drivers of horse drawn vehicles often jeered at early auto enthusiasts as they stood by their broken down cars. A favourite catcall was, "Get a horse!"

Scenario 5

When railroads in the 1950s began to change from steam to diesel, the position of fireman was no longer needed. In older steam locomotives, the fireman was responsible for shoveling coal into the boiler furnace, but diesels had no boiler or furnace. However, railroad workers resisted any efforts to eliminate the obsolete job. They even justified the position by claiming that the fireman was needed for safety reasons.

4. A theme common in all of the scenarios is that technological change is

A. extremely disruptive to most members of society

B. often resisted my some members of society

C. frequently not understood

D. harmful to society in general

5. A similar situation to that illustrated by scenario 3 would be the

A. refusal to use automated tellers at banks

B. deactivating of air bags in modern automobiles

C. preference of ground transport to air transport

D. growing of organic vegetables

6. A lesson that is **most likely** learned from the scenarios is that

A. resistance to technological change is usually unsuccessful

B. technological change is frequently not understood

C. most people do not like new and improved products

D. violence is the only way to prevent technological change

CHALLENGER QUESTION

7. In the United States, Ted Kaczynski (***the Unabomber***) launched his own campaign against technological change by mailing letter bombs to people he considered to be most responsible for the technological changes that were taking place in the 1980s and 1990s. Ted Kaczynski was acting most similarly to workers in scenarios

A. 1 and 2 **B.** 2 and 3

C. 3 and 4 **D.** 4 and 5

Use the information below to answer questions 8 and 9.

Radio, Television, and Computers

The impact of technology is sometimes hard to determine. When radio was first invented it was predicted that the new medium would make existing educational systems obsolete. This was also the belief about television. The classroom was supposed to disappear and be replaced by at-home learning systems based on the television set. While both radio and television have had an impact on learning, it is nothing like what was once predicted. Now the computer revolution has prophets once again predicting the end of conventional educational systems. It will be interesting to see whether the impact of computers will be as great as some people predict or if the traditional educational systems will remain dominant.

CHALLENGER QUESTION

8. According to the information above, predictions about the impact of technology are

A. not always based on fact

B. frequently overly pessimistic

C. based on personal biases

D. often not accurate

9. The information above seems to infer that

A. even major technological developments may have had only a slight influence on existing institutions

B. radio, television, and computers have not contributed much to human development

C. technological change sometimes has unexpected effects

D. society may not use technological breakthroughs wisely

Use the cartoon below to answer question 10.

"He's a great customer, but he's very thrifty. He wants us to E-mail five tons of freight to Cleveland."

10. The humour in the cartoon stems from the fact that advances in technology

A. do not always save money

B. are not always understood

C. are sometimes difficult to implement

D. may have unexpected uses

Use the cartoon below to answer questions 11 to 14.

"You're in luck. We have two openings, so I'm hiring you for both of them."

CHALLENGER QUESTION

11. The modern trend that refers to the use of computers to control and supervise other machines is
    - **A.** mechanization
    - **B.** automation
    - **C.** cybernation
    - **D.** industrialization

12. A person concerned about the protection of workers' rights would react to the cartoon by suggesting that
    - **A.** governments protect workers by not allowing them to be replaced by machines
    - **B.** workers receive a level of training that would allow them to use the new technology
    - **C.** governments modernize by raising their level of technology
    - **D.** technological improvements be promoted to improve efficiency

13. An opponent of technological change would respond to the cartoon by pointing out that
    - **A.** machines lack the human qualities most people prefer
    - **B.** new technology invariably leads to job losses
    - **C.** machines rarely perform tasks as well as people
    - **D.** technological change is expensive to implement

14. A supporter of computer technology would respond to the cartoon by pointing out that
    - **A.** technological change cannot be stopped
    - **B.** new technologies require fewer workers
    - **C.** technological change creates numerous benefits for society
    - **D.** modern companies make larger profits

Use the information below to answer questions 15 to 19.

Source 1

When people are taught about technological change, its sensational aspect is always emphasized. What most people do not understand is that a good deal of change is not harmful in any way. It simply makes life more convenient and enjoyable. An example of such change is the development of photography in the 19th century. Fearmongers predicted that photography would mean the end to the art of painting and the commercial artist. No such thing happened. As a matter of fact, both commercial and artistic painting is stronger than ever before.

Source 2

Dramatic change, such as the development of nuclear weapons, is always emphasized by the history books. As a result, that is what most people think of when they contemplate technological change. The truth is that many developments occur with so little disruption to society that they go almost unnoticed. How many people, for example, complain about steel belted radial tires or the use of energy saving appliances?

Source 3

Change is always disruptive because most people do not like change. As a matter of fact, the word change is often hidden behind the word progress, a word that has more favourable connotations. Most people are unwilling to oppose progress because such change is supposed to be good. As a result, in the name of progress the Earth's atmosphere has been poisoned and damaged, and people have been crowded into the unhealthy environment of large cities.

Source 4

An example of a major technological change that was not at all disruptive was the development of the motion picture industry. It is true that this was a widespread change, but was it especially disruptive or harmful? Although the impact of this change was somewhat overdramatized, it was mostly beneficial. Some people did lose their jobs, most noticeably those who worked in live theatre and music halls. However, these people were entertainers anyway, and many of them simply found jobs making movies. In addition, thousands of new jobs were created in the new industry. One only has to look at the credits at the end of a film to get some idea of just how many different new jobs were created.

Source 5

Let's look at some of the wonderful innovations that have been brought upon us without our consent. TV dinners – tasteless, over-packaged, chemically enhanced food; portable listening devices that damage the hearing of the user; overpowered recreational vehicles that are dangerous to the user, the environment, and innocent bystanders; and such toys as lawn darts, which regularly ended up embedded in children. These examples are but a few of the totally useless and harmful inventions that have been created without any demand whatsoever.

CHALLENGER QUESTION

15. The various sources are divided over the

A. value and necessity of technological change

B. cause and importance of technological change

C. importance of technological change

D. need for technological change

16. That the impact of technological change is overly dramatized is indicated in sources

A. 1, 2, and 3 **B.** 1, 2, and 4

C. 3, 4, and 5 **D.** 2, 3, and 4

CHALLENGER QUESTION

17. The harmful effects of technological change are emphasized in sources

A. 1 and 2 **B.** 2 and 3

C. 3 and 4 **D.** 3 and 5

18. According to source 3, technological change often takes place because

A. there is a conspiracy to force change on society

B. members of society do not understand the consequences of change

C. people are pressured into believing that change is good

D. people are unaware that change is taking place

19. The point being made by source 4 is that

A. major technological change may occur without any real harm to society

B. technological change is usually not a disruptive force in human development

C. the entertainment industry has greatly benefited humanity

D. the motion picture industry had very little impact on society

THE MIXED ECONOMY

Use the information below to answer questions 20 to 23.

Source 1
Ivan stared uncomprehendingly at his supervisor. "Do you understand me, comrade?" said the supervisor. "Your position is terminated. You no longer work here. The factory has too many workers. You and many others will have to find work elsewhere."

Unable to speak, Ivan turned away. What would he do? He had always worked at the factory. Then, he began to get angry. So, this is what the government had meant by reform! His job had been taken away!

Source 2
Jim put his hand on Bob's shoulder. "Sorry son, but we don't need you right now. The economy is really slowing down and we simply have too many hands. If we need you in the future, we'll give you a call."

Source 3
"Sorry Olaf, but with the modernization of the plant your job is gone." Olaf nodded and Sven continued. "The government is offering job retraining in five areas. Select one and you should be back in the work force in about a year. Of course, you will receive 90% of your old wage until you are retrained.

Source 4
"Hey kid, why don't you get a real job?" Jerry just smiled and kept playing his guitar. He'd learned to ignore the taunts of passers-by. He had spent 10 months last year looking for a "real job." Now, he spent eight or nine hours each day playing his guitar on the sidewalk. Not a "real job," but it paid the rent.

20. The comments **most likely** made by proponents of a market economy are found in sources

A. 1 and 2

B. 2 and 3

C. 3 and 4

D. 2 and 4

CHALLENGER QUESTION

21. The comments that **most likely** depict a person who was a victim of Mikhail Gorbachev's policy of *Perestroika* are found in source

A. 1 **B.** 2

C. 3 **D.** 4

22. The individual who became a victim of the business cycle in an unregulated capitalist system is **most likely** described in source

A. 1

B. 2

C. 3

D. 4

23. The characteristics of a socialist mixed economy are depicted in the scenario in source

A. 1

B. 2

C. 3

D. 4

Use the information below to answer questions 24 to 28.

Scenario 1
"Disgusting mess isn't it?" said Arnold with a wave of his hand toward the frothing filth spilling out of a large pipe. William nodded. "What is it?" he asked.
"Mostly water, some acidic components, and a few heavy metals," responded Arnold.
"Sounds like fairly nasty stuff. Is there anything we can do about it?"
"Oh sure. The question is do we want to? We could always clean it up, but it's actually cheaper to pay the fines than install proper recycling equipment and, of course, there is a very good chance that we won't get caught."

Scenario 2
Svetlana was sick. Her whole family was sick. Little Dmitri had a terrible rash. Nothing the local clinic gave him seemed to make any difference. Svetlana's husband, Ivan, had not worked for three months. He was simply too weak and tired. Svetlana believed that the air around the factory was not safe, but there wasn't much that she could do about it. Her family couldn't move. Both she and Ivan would lose their jobs. Where would they go? Housing wasn't available everywhere. It had been a two-year wait to get into their housing complex. If only it hadn't been downwind of the factory.

Scenario 3
"The court imposes a fine of $10 million on the company. In addition, the company is given two years to clean up its factory site and install proper anti-pollution equipment." The judge paused in her statement. George Spaulding breathed a sigh of relief. $10 million, that was a big fine, but the company had saved ten times that amount in its illegal dumping of pollutants. As for the cleanup order, well, the company could probably ignore that, the same way it had ignored the others.

The judge continued. "Mr. Spaulding!" The judge was looking straight at him. "In light of your company's terrible record, I sentence you to 30 months in prison. I will suspend the final 24 months if I am convinced that your company is complying with the decision of this court." George went absolutely white. Prison! He hadn't expected that! It wasn't fair. All his company had done was mess up the environment a little.

Scenario 4
Fred checked over the cost analysis of the environmental plan.

Initial cost of the anti-pollution equipment	$30 million
Yearly cost of maintaining and running the equipment	$ 5 million
TOTAL	$35 million
Recovered reusable industrial chemicals each year	$20 million
Reduced water treatment costs each year	$ 8 million
Savings from improved plant efficiency each year	$10 million
Improved public relations	$??

Fred smiled. Who would have guessed that it was actually possible to make a profit out of cleaning up your act? Not to mention the improved company image and a reduction in the number of days of work missed by employees. Now that the plant was cleaner, workers didn't mind coming to work any more.

CHALLENGER QUESTION

24. The issue that all of the scenarios have in common is

A. What is the best way to deal with pollution?

B. What are some the problems associated with pollution caused by businesses ?

C. What is the human and economic cost of pollution?

D. What is an appropriate penalty for polluting the environment?

25. Of the four scenarios, the one that would have come from people living in a centrally planned economy is found in scenario

A. 1

B. 2

C. 3

D. 4

26. Which scenarios indicate that without proper enforcement there can be no improvement in environmental standards?

A. Scenarios 2 and 4

B. Scenarios 1, 2 and 3

C. Scenarios 2, 3 and 4

D. Scenarios 1 and 4

27. Which scenario indicates that a cleaner environment need not be a money-losing proposition?

A. Scenario 1

B. Scenario 2

C. Scenario 3

D. Scenario 4

28. Which two scenarios indicate that criminal penalties may be required for proper enforcement of environmental laws?

A. Scenarios 1 and 2

B. Scenarios 2 and 3

C. Scenarios 3 and 4

D. Scenarios 1 and 3

Use the information below to answer questions 29 to 33.

Source 1
Sonya waited patiently in line. When she had first seen the line, she had gotten into it without checking to find out what was waiting at the other end. If she had taken time to check, she would have found herself much further back. She now knew that the line up was for fresh strawberries. A collective farm had trucked in a load this morning. She hoped the store would not run out of strawberries before she had a chance to buy some.

Source 2
Cliff loved garage sales. Sometimes, he received some really good bargains. Mostly, there was only junk for sale, but every now and then he picked up something really valuable. However, it was buyer beware, there were no refunds in this business.

Source 3
Boomtown! There were jobs aplenty. The problem was that Rob couldn't find any place to live that he could afford. Rents were so high that his minimum wage job didn't pay enough for him to cover the rent and also buy food.

Source 4
Sonya waited for her change. Drug prices were certainly high and she needed quite a few different medications. Thank goodness the government controlled most drug prices. Prices for uncontrolled drugs were incredibly high.

Source 5
The maize crop was coming along very well. The rains had been good this year and had come on time. Kwame optimistically forecast that there would be a large enough harvest to feed his family and provide a small surplus that he could take to market.

29. The situation that could occur in a mixed economy is found in source

A. 1 **B.** 2

C. 3 **D.** 4

30. The situation that could occur in a traditional economy is found in source

A. 1 **B.** 2
C. 3 **D.** 4

31. The situation that could occur in a centrally planned economy is found in source

A. 1 **B.** 3
C. 4 **D.** 5

32. The situation that could occur in a market economy is found in source

A. 1 **B.** 3
C. 4 **D.** 5

33. Which of the various sources depict an economic system in which most of the products produced are consumed by the producer?

A. Source 2 **B.** Source 3
C. Source 4 **D.** Source 5

Use the cartoon below to answer questions 34 to 37.

CHALLENGER QUESTION

34. The cartoon illustrates that the problem in a market economy is that

A. not everyone shares in its economic success

B. some people are too lazy to work

C. not everyone can afford to purchase goods

D. levels of income may vary from person to person

35. In dealing with the problem illustrated in the cartoon, a government that favours a mixed economy would

A. lower interest rates and decrease government spending

B. increase taxes on the wealthy and increase spending on social services

C. nationalize all privately owned businesses

D. lower taxes on all segments of society

36. A supporter of central planning would deal with the problem shown in the cartoon by

A. increasing the amount of government control over the economy

B. slowing down the economy through increased government spending

C. creating work camps to provide temporary employment

D. reducing welfare benefits to force the unemployed back to work

37. A supporter of the market system would attempt to deal with the situation illustrated in the cartoon by reducing

A. government subsidies to big business

B. taxes on the wealthy to further stimulate the economy

C. the number of days required to qualify for unemployment benefits

D. government orders to private industry

Use the information below to answer questions 38 to 40.

Advantages of a Mixed Economy	Weaknesses of a Mixed Economy
1. Allows rapid growth due to the strength of the market system	1. Government regulation may limit economic growth
2. Citizens are protected by a network of social services	2. High levels of taxation to pay for social services
3. Economic planning allows governments to regulate growth	3. Over-regulation of the economy may interfere with entrepreneurs
4. The gap between rich and poor is reduced	4. Businesses and entrepreneurs may move elsewhere in search of a more favourable business environment

CHALLENGER QUESTION

38. The above information would seem to indicate that in a mixed economy

A. economic growth is slower than in the market economy

B. entrepreneurial freedom is sacrificed for social security and equality

C. government involvement tends to over emphasize the importance of the market system

D. lack of government control may reduce social security

39. The aspect of a mixed economy to which a supporter of a market economy would object **most** strongly would be

A. government planning and regulation

B. attempts to eliminate poverty

C. promotion of industrial infrastructure

D. provision of public schools and other social services

40. A supporter of a mixed economy would **most likely** justify the higher level of taxation present in most mixed economies by pointing out that

A. such policies promote economic and social equality

B. persons opposed to such policies could always move to other countries

C. those persons who oppose such policies do so for selfish reasons

D. taxes benefit the rich as well as the poor

41. The government of a mixed economy would respond to increasing levels of unemployment by

A. increasing taxes and raising interest rates

B. attempting to balance the budget by cutting back government spending

C. increasing spending on social programs and public works

D. reducing taxes on foreign goods

42. A supporter of a mixed economy would justify such programs as public schools, Medicare, Employment Insurance, the Child Tax Credit, and welfare by pointing out that

A. such programs lower crime rates

B. people have a God-given right to government aid

C. even those who do not pay taxes are entitled to government services

D. such programs promote equality and help people in emergency situations

QUALITY OF LIFE

43. Supporters of a mixed economy would expect their government to react to an increase in the poverty level by

A. increasing spending on social services

B. reducing the length of time people are allowed to collect employment insurance

C. increasing grants to private businesses

D. increasing spending on schools to encourage students to stay in school longer

44. The government of a mixed economy would **most likely** react to a sharp decline in the value of its currency by

A. increasing government spending

B. increasing interest rates

C. printing more money

D. reducing government spending

CHALLENGER QUESTION

45. Which of the following government actions would only be characteristic of a government in a mixed economy?

A. Maintenance of a military to guard against foreign invasion

B. Creation and maintenance of a fire department

C. Creation and maintenance of a public education system

D. Maintenance of navigational aids to improve the safety of shipping

46. The characteristic of a centrally planned economy that a supporter of a mixed economy would find **most** objectionable would be the

A. emphasis on achieving economic equality

B. number of government owned companies

C. emphasis on planning economic development

D. lack of human rights and political freedoms

47. The characteristic of a pure market economy that a supporter of a mixed economy would find **most** objectionable would be its

A. emphasis on the production of consumer goods

B. high level of competition between businesses

C. ability to create wealth

D. large difference between rich and poor

Use the information below to answer question 48 to 52.

Source 1
The weakness of the mixed economy is that it does not leave entrepreneurs the freedom they require to adequately stimulate the economy. Instead, those people engaged in business are frustrated in their efforts by a tangle of government regulations and unnecessary restrictions. As a result, those nations that emphasize free enterprise develop much more rapidly than those that hamper the efforts of the true capitalist.

Source 2
The economies of countries that give free rein to capitalists develop more rapidly. There is ample statistical data to support this claim. However, there is a price to be paid for this rapid development and economic freedom. First of all, the lack of regulation in a pure market economy results in serious damage to the environment. In addition, there is a human price to pay as workers are exploited so that a few aggressive individuals can enrich themselves.

Source 3
The concept of an unregulated free enterprise system often sounds appealing, as those who favour such a system praise its advantages and point out the tiresome burdens of government regulation. However, in a modern economic system, government regulation is essential if consumers are to be protected against unscrupulous business practices. Imagine a society in which consumers were totally at the mercy of the entrepreneur. How many shoddy and even dangerous products would be passed off onto the unwary buyer?

Source 4
What is required in a modern economy is not an absence of government regulation, but a system in which the business community is free to create new wealth while controlled by safeguards that protect society in general. Such a society would ensure that consumers and workers are protected from the perils of unregulated capitalism. In addition, the average citizen would share in the wealth created by the entrepreneurial class.

CHALLENGER QUESTION

48. The issue of concern to all of the sources is

A. the most effective way to stimulate the modern economy

B. the extent that government should involve itself in the economy

C. protecting workers from the hazards of capitalism

D. finding an economic system that is most capable of creating wealth

49. The accusation that a mixed economy stifles the efforts of entrepreneurs is made in source

A. 1

B. 2

C. 3

D. 4

50. The sources that are supportive of the mixed economy do so on the grounds that the mixed economy

A. is more effective at generating wealth than the market economy

B. provides for the protection of the public

C. prevents businessmen from making too much money

D. eliminates poverty and promotes equality

51. The source that believes the mixed economy is necessary in order to protect the environment is

A. Source 1

B. Source 2

C. Source 3

D. Source 4

52. The source that states that the mixed economy allows all citizens to share in the wealth of society is

A. Source 1

B. Source 2

C. Source 3

D. Source 4

53. Which of the following government actions is **most** characteristic of a mixed economy?

A. The government regulates wages and prices of goods.

B. The government allows supply and demand to control the price of both labour and goods.

C. The government establishes a minimum wage but does not regulate the price of goods.

D. The government regulates both the supply of labour and the wages workers are paid.

54. Which of the following actions is **most** characteristic of the way government deals with goods and services in a mixed economy?

A. The government allows the market to decide what goods and services are provided.

B. The government decides what goods and services are provided.

C. The government and the private sector both provide goods and services.

D. The government provides all goods and services.

CHALLENGER QUESTION

55. Which of the following services would the government of a mixed economy **most** likely provide?

A. Pharmaceutical supplies

B. Automobile dealerships

C. Public schooling

D. Security guard services

56. Which of the following actions are **most** characteristic of a mixed economy?

A. The quality of goods and services is determined by the provider of the goods and services.

B. Goods and services are subject to government regulation to ensure quality.

C. Consumers determine the quality of goods and services through their buying habits.

D. Goods and services are manufactured by the government to ensure quality.

57. In order to ensure the least amount of unemployment, the government of a mixed economy would

A. sell off government owned businesses

B. increase the number of government owned corporations

C. reduce government spending

D. attempt to stimulate the private sector through tax cuts

ANSWERS AND SOLUTIONS
ECONOMIC GROWTH: USA

1.	D	14.	D	27.	C	40.	A	53.	D
2.	A	15.	B	28.	D	41.	A	54.	C
3.	B	16.	A	29.	B	42.	C	55.	C
4.	C	17.	C	30.	D	43.	C	56.	B
5.	C	18.	C	31.	D	44.	D	57.	D
6.	B	19.	D	32.	C	45.	C	58.	A
7.	D	20.	C	33.	C	46.	D	59.	A
8.	C	21.	A	34.	A	47.	A	60.	C
9.	B	22.	B	35.	D	48.	A	61.	D
10.	B	23.	B	36.	B	49.	B	62.	A
11.	C	24.	B	37.	B	50.	A		
12.	C	25.	C	38.	D	51.	C		
13.	B	26.	B	39.	C	52.	A		

CHANGES CAUSED BY INDUSTRIALIZATION

1. D

A. Scientific developments led to changes in technology, but many of these were not realized until the Industrial Revolution in England was already under way.

B. The English economy was considered about as modern as any economy of the day.

C. Overseas trade eventually provided markets for English goods, but was not critical to the development of the Industrial Revolution in England.

D. Without the Agricultural Revolution, there would have been no Industrial Revolution.

2. A

A. The flying shuttle, invented by John Kay, resulted in an increase in the demand for spun wool and cotton.

B. The water frame, developed by Richard Arkwright, necessitated the placing of spinning machines in water-powered mills.

C. The spinning jenny, invented by James Hargreaves, solved the problem of providing spun cotton that had been previously provided by the flying shuttle.

D. The power loom, invented by Edmund Cartwright, solved the problem of keeping up with the new spinning machines.

3. B

A. Towns developed around the new industries rather than the other way around.

B. Water-powered mills were critical to the development of the textile industry.

C. Although important for shipping, most ports had no source of power.

D. The movement of industry to coal fields followed after the textile industry was already established.

4. C

A. Domestic markets were more important to the development of American industry than European markets.

B. Raw materials for the textile industry were located in the southern United States.

C. The numerous small rivers and streams flowing through the New England region provided ample power for the new textile industry.

D. Although transport was important, the proximity to waterpower was more important factor in the development of American industry.

5. C

A. The type of crop produced is not referred to as productivity.

B. The length of time it takes to plant a field may affect productivity, but is itself not called productivity.

C. Productivity refers to the output per person.

D. The number of animals may affect productivity, but itself is not called productivity.

6. B

A. Compared to farmers in other parts of Europe, English farmers were not heavily taxed.

B. The small size and scattered nature of pre-Agricultural Revolution farms is emphasized in the source.

C. Machinery was almost non-existent, and was thus not really a factor in English farming.

D. Although poorly educated, there was little English farmers could have done to improve their output even if they had known how to do so.

7. D

A. Prior to the Agricultural Revolution, most farm production was used to feed the farmer and his family. Only a small surplus was sold.

B. England's agricultural production was so low that there were only a few products produced for export.

C. Taxation prior to the Industrial Revolution was primarily on a few consumer products such as beer and ale, or on imports in the form of customs duties.

D. About 80% of the goods produced on most farms were consumed by the farmer and his family. Very little was left to sell.

8. C

A. By the standards of the day, rents in 18th century England were not high. In addition, they were fixed by law.

B. A decline in soil fertility would actually have forced farmers to change.

C. An important factor in the reluctance of many farmers to change their farming techniques was fear of starving to death if an experimental technique failed.

D. Although mechanization was low, it did not slow change because on most farms mechanization was not a factor.

9. B

A. Overseas trade had very little impact on the improvement of agriculture.

B. The Enclosure Movement resulted in larger, more efficient farms, which led to numerous scientific developments in agriculture.

C. Although important, this development took place only after the Enclosure Movement had paved the way for agricultural innovation.

D. Innovations in agriculture actually resulted in a decrease in the number of farmers.

10. B

A. Neither innovations in manufacturing nor in acquiring abundant raw materials would have had any influence on the development of markets for goods.

B. England's growing population and the existence of markets in overseas colonies provided important markets for manufactured goods.

C. Internal unity and political stability created an environment conducive to industrial development. However, this environment did not create any new markets for goods.

D. The influence of a strong entrepreneurial class as well as improvements in transportation made it possible for industrial development to proceed. However, these factors alone did not create any new markets.

11. C

A. Improvements in transport and an overseas empire helped England develop industrially, but were not factors in its political unity.

B. Manufacturing innovations and a strong entrepreneurial class aided in England's industrial development, but did not aid in its political development.

C. A lack of internal divisions and a stable government were key factors in England's industrial development, as trade barriers and fear of civil war were eliminated.

D. A surplus of labour and an overseas empire helped to boost industrial development, but did not promote its political unity.

12. C

A. None of the references in the question deal with manufacturing techniques.

B. Internal unity was aided by developments in transportation, but improved transport was not the only factor in Britain's unity.

C. All of the references in the question deal with transportation.

D. England's overseas empire had very little effect on the development of transport in England.

13. B

A. None of the listed factors apply to technical improvements.

B. All of the factors listed apply to technical improvements.

C. None of the factors listed apply to technical improvements.

D. Although factor 1 fits the question, factors 3 and 6 do not.

14. D

A. This factor has very little to do with the development of the iron industry.

B. This factor has very little to do with the development of the iron industry.

C. This factor has very little to do with the development of the iron industry.

D. Clearly, abundant supplies of coal and iron fit the question precisely.

15. B

A. Crop variety did increase somewhat during the Agricultural Revolution, but not significantly.

B. Food production increased in Britain to the point where the country could feed its expanding population for the next century.

C. Due to increased efficiency, the cost of food actually decreased in Britain during this time period.

D. The amount of land available for farming did increase somewhat during the Agricultural Revolution, but this was not due to the efforts of the three individuals in the sources.

16. A

A. The modernization of agriculture during the 18th and 19th centuries was known as the Agricultural Revolution.

B. The Scientific Revolution occurred in the 16th and 17th centuries and preceded the Agricultural Revolution.

C. There really is no such age as the Age of Machines, but if there was, it would be the same as the Industrial Revolution.

D. The Commercial Revolution occurred during the Age of Exploration of the 16th and 17th centuries.

17. C

A. For a large part of this time period, the cost of farm production steadily decreased.

B. Farm size during this time period has steadily increased.

C. This trend continues even today. Farmers now make up only about five percent of the population.

D. Although this is true in some regions, improved farming techniques have actually improved soil fertility in some regions.

18. C

A. A lack of overseas markets was never much of a problem for British industry.

B. As its population grew, Britain's domestic market grew larger and stronger.

C. Without the modernization of agriculture, Britain would not have had enough food to feed its growing population.

D. During the time period, demand for machinery increased as farms grew larger and more efficient.

19. D

A. Britain's command of the sea meant that overseas trade was rarely seriously disrupted by pirates or military conflict.

B. Although this was true during the early part of its industrial development, Britain actually lowered tariffs as the 19th century progressed.

C. Government subsidies played a very small part in the development of British agriculture during its industrial development.

D. During this time period, Britain's population grew rapidly.

20. C

A. In order to protect American businesses from foreign competition, there were very high taxes on foreign goods.

B. Until the development of the railroad, transport in the United States was very far from being advanced.

C. Protection from foreign competition gave weak American industries a chance to compete against the much more highly developed industrial nations of Europe.

D. Although the American government has always strongly favoured free enterprise, it has intervened almost continually in the American economy in the interest of aiding American business.

21. A.

A. Railroads were especially important in developing the huge resource potential of the United States and tying together the enormous country.

B. Although the riverboat had tremendous influence on transportation and communication along the United States' major river systems, it did not have the same impact as that of the railroad.

C. Canal building was important during the industrial development of the United States, but was outshone by the more flexible and versatile railroad.

D. Coastal shipping was critical during the early years of American industrial development, but was not capable of having any real impact on the development of the vast frontier.

22. B

A. Although very romantic, the Pony Express was not a very important development in the history of the United States, as it lasted only two years and was rendered obsolete by the development of the telegraph.

B. The building of the railroad across the United States linked the country from coast to coast and made possible the development of vast regions of the country.

C. Port improvements were important, but took place gradually and did not have the impact on development that the railroad did.

D. An important development in transportation and communication, the Panama Canal was not opened until after the United States was already the world's foremost industrial power.

23. B.

A. Although some armaments have triggers, the armament industry does not necessarily qualify as a trigger industry.

B. A trigger industry is one that indeed does result in a number of other economic developments. An example of such an industry was the textile industry in Britain and the construction of railroads in both Britain and the United states.

C. Trigger industries by their very nature have influence in many areas of the economy.

D. There are numerous forms of trigger industries, but attempts to copy an existing trigger industry are rare or non-existent. Trigger industries tend to develop almost spontaneously.

THE MARKET ECONOMY

24. B

A. The principle of supply and demand controls the price of goods in a market economy. Case study 1 is an example of a businessman falling to superior competition.

B. Competition is the force in a market economy that creates better products, better prices, and better services. Businesses that cannot compete are driven out of business.

C. Individualism is what makes people set up their own businesses in an effort to succeed. The case study does not emphasize individualism as much as it does the factor of competition.

D. Case study 1 does illustrate private ownership, but it is not emphasized as the main idea of the study.

25. C

A. Case study 2 illustrates the virtues of hard work in a market system. Case study 3 illustrates competition.

B. Case study 4 illustrates innovation. An entrepreneur has come up with a new idea. Case study 3 illustrates competition.

C. Case study 4 illustrates innovation and case study 5 shows an ability to adapt to increased competition

D. Case studies 1 and 2 are opposites. Case study 1 illustrates failure to compete successfully and case study 2 illustrates the virtues of hard work.

26. B

A. The emphasis in case study 1 is the effects of competition, but this case illustrates the problem of the small businessman when facing competition from a large competitor.

B. Case study 2 clearly illustrates that hard work can lead to success.

C. The emphasis in case study 3 is also that of competition, but this case illustrates the effects of oversupply on a business.

D. Case study 4 emphasizes innovation.

27. C

A. The emphasis in case study 1 is the effects of competition.

B. Case study 2 shows that hard work can lead to success.

C. Case study 3 illustrates an example of oversupply.

D. Case study 4 emphasizes innovation.

28. D

A. Case study 2 does not illustrate supply and demand, it illustrates that hard work and determination can lead to success.

B. Public ownership refers to government owned businesses. There is no hint of that in the case study.

C. Freedom of choice is a phrase that is usually applied to consumers of goods and services rather than to those who supply them.

D. Hard work and individual initiative – the willingness to take matters into one's own hands – is illustrated in the example.

29. B

A. Increasing taxes would likely result in a slowdown in the economy, but would be unlikely to influence the value of the dollar.

B. Persons who favour free enterprise prefer an absence of government involvement in the economy. This answer fits that characteristic.

C. Raising interest rates would probably increase the value of the dollar, but would be interference in the economy.

D. Lowering interest rates would decrease the value of the dollar even further because of investors selling off the dollar for better investment.

30. D

A. Establishment of environmental standards would be considered by many to be interference in the market system.

B. Unfortunately, in an unregulated market economy, monopolies tend to develop.

C. In a pure market system, the poor are expected to fend for themselves.

D. A pure market system is supposed to operate without government involvement.

31. D

A. Private ownership of land is an important characteristic of the market economy, but by itself does not affect price, quality, or innovation.

B. Individual initiative is very important in the market economy, but does not necessarily lead to improvements in price and quality or innovation.

C. Consumerism is the desire to acquire goods. It has little or no influence on price, quality and innovation.

D. Competition is the overwhelmingly important factor in determining price, quality, and innovation. Without competition, the market economy would not function.

32. C

A. John D. Rockefeller was the most important figure in the development of the early oil industry.

B. Charles Hall was the inventor of the Hall Process for the extraction of aluminum from bauxite.

C. Adam Smith is considered the father of the capital system. His book, *The Wealth Of Nations*, became the Bible of the capitalist system.

D. Ray Kroc was the founder of the modern chain of fast food restaurants known as McDonald's.

33. C

A. The Board of Directors controls the operation of a modern company, but does not necessarily own the company.

B. Some workers in a company may own shares in the business, but only if they choose to buy them.

C. The bulk of shares in most modern corporations is owned by millions of shareholders who do not work for or direct the operations of the company.

D. As stated in A and B, workers and members of the Board of Directors usually do not own enough shares to have ownership of the company.

34. A

A. Without the consumer to create demand in a market economy, there would be little or no economic activity.

B. Competition between producers is more important than the choices made by consumers in determining the quality of goods.

C. Consumers can help maintain levels of competition in a market economy, but government legislation regulating or outlawing monopolies may be just as important in maintaining levels of competition between businesses.

D. In a market economy, levels of production are determined by the demand for a product.

35. D.

A. Government regulated central banks are characteristic of most modern mixed or centrally planned economies, but are not typical of a model market economy.

B. An attempt by a number of banks to control interest rates would be considered a distortion of the free market.

C. The printing of money is supposed to keep up with the expansion of the economy, but not influence interest rates.

D. Demand for credit is supposed to determine high or low interest rates in a market economy. High demand would force up interest rates, low demand would cause rates to fall.

36. B

A. Not one of the speakers suggests that the market economy be regulated, although several complain about its lack of fairness.

B. The lack of balance of the market economy is commented on by three of the five speakers.

C. None of the speakers seems to feel that prices in a market system are unfair.

D. There is a concern that some of the goods produced in a market economy may not be desirable, but there is little concern among the speakers that too many goods are produced.

37. B

A. Speaker 1 is strongly supportive of almost all aspects of the market economy.

B. Speaker 2 clearly states that many products that are produced are wasteful and useless.

C. The main concern of Speaker 3 is the unequal distribution of wealth in a market economy.

D. Speaker 4 is primarily concerned with the distortion of values that occurs in a market economy.

38. D

A. Although Speaker 2 does not strongly favour the market economy, he says little about the inequality that develops in a market system.

B. Speaker 3 is concerned only with the negative effects of inequality in the market economy.

C. Speaker 4 comments about the lack of fairness in the market system, but in no way supports this lack of equality.

D. Speaker 5 clearly believes that inequality is a good thing and makes no apologies for the differences in incomes that develop in a market economy.

39. C

A. Speaker 1 clearly sees nothing harmful about the market economy.

B. Speaker 2 is primarily concerned about the pollution and wastefulness of the market economy.

C. Speaker 4 is clearly concerned that many people who are heavily rewarded in a market economy do not deserve the wealth that they accumulate, and thus distort peoples' values about what is important and what is not.

D. Speaker 5 supports the inequities that develop in the market economy.

40. A

A. Speaker 1 leaves no doubt that he believes the market economy is an almost perfect system.

B. Speaker 2 is more critical of the market system than supportive.

C. Speaker 4 has little to say in support of the market economy.

D. Speaker 5 supports the market system strongly, but does not state as clearly as speaker 1 that he considers it a perfect system.

41. A

A. Oil and gas consumption is not only an example of the use of a declining resource, but also adds to pollution problems.

B. Hydroelectric power is considered a renewable resource and therefore is not considered to be as much of a problem as other types of resource use.

C. Solar panels, like hydroelectric power, make use of a renewable resource.

D. Environmentalists do not consider consumption of basic food products wasteful.

42. C

A. Speaker 1 is concerned about the fact that a great deal of advertising lies about or exaggerates the virtues of a product.

B. Speaker 2 supports advertising because without it consumers would lack information about new products.

C. Speaker 3 points out that advertising makes modern mass production possible by increasing the demand for a product.

D. Speaker 5 is concerned about the wasteful attitudes promoted by advertising.

43. C

A Speaker 1 clearly points out the problems of the lack of truth in advertising, but speaker 2 is strongly supportive of the advertising industry.

B. Speaker 3 supports advertising. Speaker 4 condemns it.

C. Speakers 1 and 4 clearly believe that advertising causes serious problems for society by distorting the truth about products.

D. Speakers 2 and 3 are both supportive of advertising.

44. D

A. Speaker 1 is most concerned about the lack of truth in advertising, but makes no reference to matters of health.

B. Speaker 2 is entirely positive about advertising.

C. Speaker 3 is also entirely supportive of advertising.

D. Speaker 4 points out that consumers are encouraged to buy unhealthy products such as tobacco and alcohol.

45. C

A. Speaker 1 makes no reference to the cost of products.

B. Speaker 2 also makes no reference to the cost of products.

C. Speaker 3 clearly points out that advertising reduces the cost of products to the consumer.

D. Speaker 4 is entirely negative about the value of advertising.

46. D

A. This actually supports the speaker because price increases force people to use their resources more carefully.

B. Finding new ways of using resources may or may not result in their being used more wisely. This answer neither supports nor attacks the evidence.

C. Buying of bulk food is not necessarily a wise or unwise use of resources.

D. Waste disposal clearly points to a problem in wise use of resources. If resources were used wisely, waste would not be a significant problem.

47. A

A. Because consumers have the freedom to choose the goods that they want, they can greatly influence the types of goods that are provided to them.

B. Although this may be due to consumer influence, it is not as clearly stated as in Point A.

C. The flexibility of the market system is not related to consumer choice.

D. Monetary rewards are not related to freedom of choice.

48. A

A. Price increases in the price of any product result in it being used more wisely.

B. Increased exploration may result in more of a product being discovered, but not necessarily in it being used more wisely.

C. Hoarding of a product would drive up the price of the product and perhaps cause people to use it more wisely, but more than likely would simply result in the limited supply being made available to those with the most money.

D. Price fluctuations such as those for fruits and vegetables are temporary and do not have a major impact on resource use.

49. B

A. The world recession of the 1970s was an example of the temporary inability of the world economy to adapt to a sudden change in the availability of a critical resource.

B. The switch to alternative fuels in the 1970s such as wood, solar, and wind power was an example of the flexibility of the market economy.

C. Use of gas fireplaces actually increases the use of fossil fuels rather than replacing them.

D. New uses for petroleum products would increase not decrease their use.

50. A

A. For many people the obsession with making money creates serious problems for them and for other members of society.

B. Encouragement of hard work certainly rates as an advantage of the market economy and not a disadvantage.

C. Loyalty to an employer is certainly not a disadvantage provided the employee is treated fairly.

D. This is considered one of the greatest strengths of the market economy.

51. C

A. Reward for hard work is considered an advantage of the market economy.

B. Freedom of choice is considered one of the greatest strengths of the market economy.

C. The salaries paid to professional athletes are considered a distortion of values by many.

D. Rewarding developers of new products is considered a strength of the market economy.

52. A

A. Although large businesses may create distortions in the market system, it is true that they grow large because their products are in demand.

B. Elimination of competition would actually weaken the market system.

C. The ability of large businesses to acquire raw materials more cheaply gives them a decided advantage over smaller businesses and may actually weaken the market system.

D. This answer has little to do with the question. It is a true statement, but it has no relevance to the question.

53. D

A. Although advertising sports such as skiing is an attempt to influence consumers, it is aimed at a particular segment of the market and is not considered harmful.

B. Alerting consumers to a sale would be considered a beneficial use of advertising.

C. Introducing a new product would also be considered a beneficial use of advertising.

D. Mass marketing of soft drinks is considered harmful because it promotes a product that is of dubious value to society.

54. C

A. Persons who have inherited their wealth are considered by many to have done nothing to deserve such wealth.

B. This would be a weak argument, because it concedes that some people do harm the environment.

C. This is the strongest argument in favour of rewarding some people more than others.

D. Although this may be true for a few, it is a difficult to justify keeping so many members of society below the poverty line.

55. C

A. An intelligent consumer can overcome attempted manipulation. Therefore, although this is a serious problem for many, it is not considered as serious as some other aspects of the market economy.

B. Distortion of social values is a problem for many members of the market economy. However, to the average member of society this is not the most serious problem generated by the market economy.

C. The boom and bust cycle has a powerful influence on the average member of a market economy. Any person who has ever experienced a serious economic slump, with its high rate of unemployment and economic uncertainty, may remember the effects for the rest of his life.

D. Most members of a market economy believe that differences in wealth are justified.

56. B

A. Although size gives a competitive advantage, even large corporations are subject to competition from other large corporations.

B. Corporations were originally created for exactly this reason. Very large corporations are capable of raising millions or even hundreds of millions of dollars for expansion.

C. Although this is an important characteristic of many large businesses, it is tied to the ability to raise capital for investment.

D. In a modern economy, the ability of large businesses to simply destroy their competition is discouraged.

57. D

A. Supporters of a market economy would consider manpower retraining programs as unnecessary government involvement in the economy.

B. Supporters of the market economy would view any government support for the unemployed as a violation of the principles of the market economy.

C. Such action was actually taken in Canada during the Great Depression, but a true supporter of the market economy would expect workers to struggle on by themselves.

D. A supporter of the market economy would expect workers to do exactly as suggested in the answer.

58. A

A. The information in the cartoon depicts a situation typical of an unregulated market economy, also known as a *laissez-faire* economy.

B. A very low level of trade and commerce characterizes a traditional economy. This is not indicated by the cartoon.

C. A command or centrally planned economy is characterized by considerable government regulation and control, which is not indicated by the cartoon.

D. A mixed economy would provide some level of protection for workers, a factor that is not indicated by the cartoon.

59. A

A. A person who supports *laissez-faire* economics believes that market forces should control the economy.

B. A supporter of *laissez-faire* economics would believe that the poor should look after themselves without any outside help.

C. Minimum wage legislation would be viewed by a supporter of the *laissez-faire* system as unnecessary interference in the economy.

D. Supporters of *laissez-faire* economics believe that unions distort the operation of the market system by giving workers too much power.

60. C

A. Capital usually refers to money, tools, machines, or other assets of a company that have value.

B. As the name implies, "land" is the land that a company owns or the natural resources on the land.

C. Labour refers to the workers. The speaker states that the workers are the ones responsible for the growth of the *Edmonton Sun.*

D. Mass production is the creation of large quantities of goods especially by using machinery.

QUALITY OF LIFE

61. D

A. The cartoon makes no reference to the amount of money people make in a market economy.

B. While people may apply for any job that they want in a market economy, this is not necessarily what the cartoon is about. Rather, it is dealing with how people with certain skills may be employed in low skilled jobs.

C. The cartoon is actually referring to the opposite: that people are sometimes employed in jobs that are inappropriate for their training.

D. This is the weakness in a market economy that the cartoon refers to. Often, people in such economies cannot find jobs that they are trained for. So, they are forced to take unskilled labour jobs.

62. A

A. The sales clerk's statement reveals that the product was not made in America. Companies often produce their goods in countries where labour costs are cheaper than local labour markets.

B. While the toy was not made in America, this does not mean that there is a lack of goods produced locally.

C. The quality of the goods is not mentioned anywhere in the cartoon.

D. Child labour is not mentioned in the cartoon.

GROW YOUR COURAGE, GROW YOUR NERVE! FACE YOUR FEARS AND CONQUER THEM. GROW YOUR SKILL GROW YOUR SIR GALLAHAD-NESS. GROW SOME CRAZY MONKEY NINJA MOJO AND HUCK THE HONKIN' FAT SCARY STUFF!
ALWAYS GROW.
GROW ALL WAYS.
ALBERTA milk
www.neverstopmilk.ca
Never Stop. Milk.™

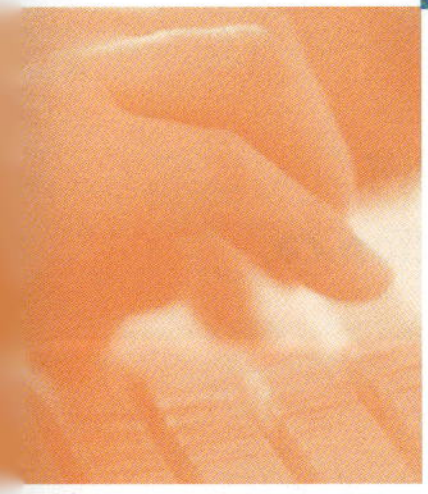

ANSWERS AND SOLUTIONS
ECONOMIC GROWTH: FORMER USSR

1.	**B**	**15.**	**B**	**29.**	**C**	**43.**	**C**	**57.**	**B**
2.	**D**	**16.**	**D**	**30.**	**A**	**44.**	**B**	**58.**	**A**
3.	**B**	**17.**	**B**	**31.**	**C**	**45.**	**D**	**59.**	**D**
4.	**D**	**18.**	**C**	**32.**	**A**	**46.**	**D**	**60.**	**A**
5.	**B**	**19.**	**D**	**33.**	**D**	**47.**	**C**	**61.**	**D**
6.	**D**	**20.**	**A**	**34.**	**C**	**48.**	**A**	**62.**	**C**
7.	**A**	**21.**	**C**	**35.**	**C**	**49.**	**D**	**63.**	**D**
8.	**B**	**22.**	**C**	**36.**	**B**	**50.**	**A**	**64.**	**A**
9.	**D**	**23.**	**A**	**37.**	**D**	**51.**	**B**	**65.**	**D**
10.	**C**	**24.**	**A**	**38.**	**A**	**52.**	**A**	**66.**	**B**
11.	**D**	**25.**	**C**	**39.**	**C**	**53.**	**D**		
12.	**C**	**26.**	**C**	**40.**	**D**	**54.**	**C**		
13.	**A**	**27.**	**A**	**41.**	**D**	**55.**	**D**		
14.	**C**	**28.**	**C**	**42.**	**D**	**56.**	**D**		

THE INFLUENCE OF GEOGRAPHY ON THE ECONOMIC DEVELOPMENT OF THE FORMER USSR

1. B

A. None of the places would be considered extremely dry.

B. Short growing seasons are found in almost all of the regions.

C. All regions would probably have winter snowfall.

D. It cannot be determined whether elevation would have a significant impact on settlement in all regions.

2. D

A. Murmansk could support limited agriculture.

B. Moscow is most suitable for human settlement.

C. Vladivostok could support limited agriculture.

D. Irkutsk has the lowest average temperature and receives limited rainfall.

3. B

A. The severe temperatures and low precipitation found in Murmansk would make agriculture almost impossible.

B. Moscow has the best combination of temperature and precipitation for agriculture.

C. Vladivostok could support agriculture, but is not as warm as Moscow.

D. Irkutsk is too cold to support agriculture.

4. D

A. Russia has vast resources in the eastern portion of the country.

B. Proximity to Western Europe did not influence Russia's original settlement patterns.

C. There are few barriers to invasion in Western Europe.

D. Most of Russia's agriculture is found in the western part of the country.

5. B

A. Source 1 deals with the problem of transport, but source 3 does not.

B. All three sources mention problems of transport.

C. Sources 3 and 4 do not mention transport problems.

D. Source 4 does not mention transport problems even though source 5 does.

6. D

A. Source 1 deals with Russia's transportation problems.

B. Source 2 deals with Russia's vast wealth of resources.

C. Source 3 deals with Russia's climate problem.

D. Source 4 deals with the impact of history on Russia.

7. A

A. Russia has over 160 different ethnic groups. Creating a nation out of such a diverse ethnic background has been very difficult.

B. Foreign invasion is dealt with in source 4.

C. Most of Russia gets adequate precipitation.

D. The effect of Russia's climate is dealt with in source 3.

8. B

A. Russia's development has been relatively slow due to the numerous obstacles to development.

B. The examples clearly indicate that Russia has progressed slowly due to numerous difficulties.

C. Russia's people are not any more backward than those of other nations, but they have faced greater obstacles to development.

D. Russia really did not develop rapidly until after the Russian Revolution of 1917.

INDUSTRIALIZATION IN PRE-REVOLUTIONARY RUSSIA

9. D

A. As stated in the reading, the peasants did receive some land.

B. The large landowners were required to sell a large part of their holdings, and thus lost control of much of their land.

C. The peasants had paid taxes before, so taxes on their land would not have especially annoyed them.

D. The fact that the peasants were required to pay for their land over a 99-year period was a source of much discontent.

10. C

A. The land the peasants farmed was not scattered, but the peasants were often required to change the areas that they farmed from year to year, which made improvements on the land difficult.

B. Although the average peasant holding was not large, it was big enough for them to survive.

C. Control of the land by the *mir* was a source of irritation, as the peasants could not truly call the land that they farmed their own.

D. Very little of the land owned by the *mir* was used for anything other than farming.

GOVERNMENT PLANNING IN RUSSIA

11. D

A. At the beginning of the war, Russia's huge reserves of manpower were considered a major advantage.

B. Compared to Germany, Russia's soldiers were poorly trained, but they fought as well as those of her other enemy, Austria-Hungary.

C. Patriotism was not something that the average Russian soldier was short of.

D. Russia's lack of a strong industrial base meant that her armies were deprived of the equipment and munitions to fight a major war.

12. C

A. Russia's generals had few illusions about the ability of the Russian armies after the disasters of the first few months of the war.

B. Russia had the largest army in the world, but her soldiers were poorly equipped.

C. Shortages of modern equipment resulted in numerous defeats for Russia during World War I. Because of the shortage of rifles, many soldiers actually went into battle armed only with bayonets.

D. Russian soldiers were better adapted than most to handle the cold Russian winters.

13. A

A. Russia's backward economy left it unable to cope with the demands of fighting a major war and looking after the basic needs of the population.

B. The upper classes did hoard goods, but this was not the most important reason for the shortage of necessities during the war.

C. Although Russia was cut off from its Western allies, it would not have been possible for these nations to supply Russia with all of the goods that she needed.

D. The Russian military, like the civilian population, was also short of critical supplies.

14. C

A. Although this is true, there is no reference to it in any of the sources.

B. This is not true, and none of the sources mention it.

C. Source 5 clearly indicates that this was a major cause for the loss of faith in the Czar and his government.

D. Russia was not prepared for a modern war, but none of the sources indicate that this was the fault of the Czar.

15. B

A. The suffering of the Russian people during World War I was such that only the removal of the Czar would satisfy their desire for change.

B. The horrors of the war eventually led to the fall of Czar Nicholas II.

C. Russia never surrendered to Germany in World War I, although it was forced to conclude a humiliating peace treaty with the Germans.

D. Although Germany gained vast amounts of Russian territory as a result of the Treaty of Brest-Litovsk, most of the territory was returned when Germany surrendered to the Allies in 1918.

16. D

A. Stalin is described in source 3.

B. Alexander Kerensky was the leader of the provisional government, which took power after the fall of the Czar. He was overthrown by Lenin in 1917.

C. Trotsky is described in source 4.

D. Lenin, the brilliant and ruthless leader of the Bolsheviks, is described in source 1.

17. B

A. Source 1 describes V.I. Lenin, the dynamic leader of the Russian Revolution.

B. Source 2 describes Karl Marx, considered the father of communist thought.

C. Source 3 describes Joseph Stalin, the eventual leader of the Soviet Union following the death of Lenin.

D. Source 4 describes Leon Trotsky, probably the most important Bolshevik leader after Lenin.

18. C

A. Lenin is described in source 1.

B. Marx is described in source 2.

C. Stalin is described in source 3.

D. Trotsky is described in source 4.

19. D

A. Lenin is described in source 1.

B. Marx is described in source 2.

C. Stalin is described in source 3.

D. Trotsky is described in source 4.

20. A

A. Lenin, described in source 1, is considered to be most responsible for the success of the revolution.

B. Marx is described in source 2.

C. Stalin is described in source 3.

D. Trotsky is described in source 4.

21. C

A. This did not happen. Under the New Economic Policy, only small to middle-sized businesses were returned to private hands. The rest remained under state control.

B. Long term planning of the Soviet economy did not occur until the late 1920s, under the leadership of Joseph Stalin.

C. The economy of the Soviet Union was in such poor shape that it was considered necessary to re-institute some aspects of capitalism in order to give the weak economy a boost.

D. Collectivization of agriculture did not occur until the First Five-Year Plan in the late 1920s.

22. C

A. The statement is accurate, but it is not the over-all theme as it is contradicted by the other sources.

B. Clearly the evidence in source 1 contradicts this answer.

C. This is the best answer. Sources 2 to 5 illustrate the price paid by Soviet citizens and source 1 indicates the success of central planning.

D. Not all of the sources deal with this concept, even though it happens to be true.

23. A

A. Source 5 clearly states that agriculture was the least successful area of Soviet development.

B. None of the sources mention anything about transportation.

C. None of the sources mention anything about mining.

D. According to source 1, energy production was one of the more successful areas of development.

24. A

A. Workers in the Soviet Union were expected to make some sacrifice for the betterment of their society.

B. The Industrial revolution was a phenomenon caused by capitalism. It is unlikely that a communist would want to compare Soviet communism with capitalistic industrialization.

C. Although this may be true, it was not supposed to be true in the workers' paradise of the Soviet Union.

D. It would be difficult to argue that all persons who suffered under central planning were enemies of the Soviet Union.

25. C

A. As indicated in source 5, agriculture was the least successful area of Soviet development.

B. If central planning was truly successful, there would have been less suffering on the part of the Soviet people.

C. The achievements of central planning indicated by source 1 are very impressive.

D. Agriculture could hardly be considered a successful example of central planning.

26. C

A. The benefits of the First Five-Year Plan were widespread and benefitted most members of the Soviet population.

B. This statement does not contain any paradox (contradiction).

C. This is the best answer. The First Five-Year Plan was achieved only at great cost to the people that it helped.

D. This statement is true, but there is no paradox here.

27. A

- **A. The process of creating a society, in which Stalin was the supreme ruler, was coined Stalinization.**
- B. The Soviet Union became an authoritarian state under communism, but this is not the most specific answer.
- C. Absolutism is a synonym for an authoritarian government, but it is also not as good an answer as alternative A.
- D. Although Stalin was a despot (absolute ruler), this is still not as good an answer as alternative A.

28. C

- A. It is unlikely that Stalin believed that so many of his victims were a threat to communism.
- B. Although this was one of the effects of Stalin's purges, it was probably not his intent to have everyone fear him.
- **C. Stalin eliminated most of his enemies (both real and imagined), thus strengthening his power and reducing his paranoia (illogical fear).**
- D. Although Stalin feared assassination, it is doubtful that he really thought it necessary to kill as many people as he did in order to feel safe.

29. C

- A. The economic impact of Stalin's purges was not as great as its political, psychological, and military impact.
- B. There was a major political impact of Stalin's purges, however, this answer does not take into account the psychological and military impact as well.
- **C. This answer encompasses all of the major effects of Stalin's reign of terror.**
- D. The Soviet Union's culture and economy may have been affected by the purges, but not as greatly as it was affected politically, psychologically, and militarily.

THE CENTRALLY PLANNED ECONOMY

30. A

- **A. Need is always the most important factor in determining what to produce under central planning.**
- B. The desires and wants of the consumer are generally ignored in a centrally planned economy.
- C. The cost of producing a product is sometimes ignored under central planning, if it is determined that society really needs the product.
- D. The profit motive is ignored in a centrally planned economy.

31. C

A. The impact on the environment would be of secondary importance in a centrally planned economy.

B. Producing the most goods for the least cost is a characteristic of the market economy, not of central planning.

C. A method of production that would benefit society most would be the choice made in a centrally planned economy.

D. Speed of production would be of secondary importance to benefitting society in a centrally planned economy.

32. A

A. Need would be the most important factor in determining who received the goods produced by a centrally planned system.

B. The ability to afford a product would not necessarily determine who would receive a product in a centrally planned system.

C. In a centrally planned system, those who could not afford a product might receive it, but only if it was thought that they really needed the product.

D. Only those who really needed a product would be thought to be most deserving in a centrally planned economy.

33. D

A. Demand would have little influence on decisions to produce a product under central planning.

B. Competition plays no part in a centrally planned economy, because there are no competing businesses.

C. Resources will be obtained in a centrally planned economy if it is determined that society needs a product badly enough.

D. How much society needs a product is the overwhelming factor in determining whether or not a product will be produced.

34. C

A. The business cycle has no influence on a centrally planned economy because there is no business cycle.

B. Demand for goods and services does not greatly influence a centrally planned economy.

C. The decisions of government planners are critical to the speed of economic growth in a centrally planned economy.

D. If central planners decided a product was needed, then it would be produced regardless of its cost. Needed raw materials would be obtained at any cost.

35. C

A. The Soviet Union was and still is one of most resource rich nations in the world.

B. The military had top priority in the Soviet Union. Its needs were always seen to first.

C. Consumer demand was always secondary in importance when it came to determining what goods to produce in the Soviet Union.

D. Demand for labour is an important consideration in all economic systems.

36. B

A. Individualism means that people are expected to look after their own affairs and not rely on anyone else.

B. The lack of competition in the Soviet Union led to the situation described in the question.

C. The right to own private property may create a situation that will lead to competition, but that still leaves B as the best answer.

D. State intervention might be responsible for the situation in the question.

37. D

A. Although national growth is important, it is not the basis of central planning.

B. In a centrally planned economy, there is usually a reduction of freedoms.

C. Personal gain is not considered important in a centrally planned system.

D. The ability to help the greatest number of people is the most important motive for central planning.

38. A

A. Because of the lack of rewards in most Soviet industries, it was very rare for workers to do any more than the minimum.

B. The huge size of government in the Soviet Union slowed economic decision making, but did not have much effect on the attitude of workers.

C. Restrictions on freedom did have an impact on the attitude of the average Soviet worker, but not as much as the lack of any material rewards.

D. Although consumer demands were ignored, this did not really affect the attitude of workers in the Soviet Union.

39. C

A. The size of government in the Soviet Union created certain inefficiencies, but these were not as serious as the government's attitude toward consumer demand.

B. The lack of freedom did not influence the shortage of consumer goods in the Soviet Union.

C. Throughout its history the Soviet Union steadfastly ignored the demands of Soviet consumers. As a result there was a serious shortage of consumer goods in the country.

D. The complexity of central planning made it difficult to satisfy consumer demand, but was not as serious as the lack of emphasis on the supplying of consumer goods.

40. D

A. The large bureaucracies in the Soviet Union often slowed decision making, but the complexity of the Soviet system was a more important factor in the example.

B. Lack of individual freedom is not a factor in the example.

C. Consumer demand is not a factor in the example.

D. The example clearly indicates the complexity of the Soviet system of central planning.

41. D

A. Disadvantage 1 makes no mention of services intended for use by the entire population.

B. Disadvantage 2 focuses on the weakness of central planning, not on its virtues.

C. Disadvantage 3 points out the successes of central planning without focusing on facilities that are in tended to benefit everyone.

D. Disadvantage 4 illustrates the strengths of central planning by using the creation of public facilities as an example.

42. D

A. Government bureaucracies may have helped cause the problems listed in the example, but not as seriously as the complexity of central planning did.

B. The lack of individual freedoms did not have much of an impact on the missing of production goals in the Soviet Union.

C. Although consumer demand was usually ignored, a more important factor in the missing of goals was the complexity of central planning.

D. As the Soviet economy evolved, it became more and more difficult for the central planners in the Soviet Union to deal with an increasingly complex economy.

43. C

A. Only source 1 depicts a market economy.

B. None of the examples depicts a traditional economy.

C. Each example illustrates one of the problems created by a shortage of consumer goods in a centrally planned economy.

D. Only sources 3 and 4 depict the sale of illegal goods in a centrally planned economy.

44. B

A. There is no indication that anyone in the example believed in the superiority of any economic system.

B. The source indicates that the person in the example is not at all familiar with the fact that in market economies merchants replace goods as they are sold.

C. There is no indication that there is any confusion over the law of supply and demand.

D. The value of the Canadian dollar would have little impact on the situation described.

45. D

A. Source 1 is not taking place in the Soviet Union.

B. Source 2 is illustrating a problem of scarcity due to planning priorities.

C. Source 3 is commenting on the problem of hoarding.

D. Source 4 is an illustration of the Black Market, which was one of the few areas where the law of supply and demand functioned in the Soviet Union.

46. D

A. This is a weak answer. It is unlikely that leaving the items in question attached to the car would cause them any harm.

B. There is no indication that Pavel's actions were motivated by scientific curiosity.

C. This is a possible answer, however, in the Soviet Union theft was a greater fear.

D. It was common in the Soviet Union to remove items that might be stolen from cars each night. Because of the shortage of replacement parts, theft of detachable items was common.

47. C

A. Source 2 is a possible answer to the question, but source 1 is clearly not taking place in the Soviet Union.

B. Source 2 deals more with the problem of theft in the Soviet Union. Although this may have been caused by shortages of goods, it is not as strong as other possible answers.

C. Sources 3 and 4 both depict situations resulting from the shortages of goods in the Soviet Union.

D. Source 3 fits the answer, but source 1 does not.

48. A

A. Taken together, the sources are arguing about whether or not central planning is a system that should be used.

B. None of the sources seems concerned about this issue. Instead all look at the larger issue of whether or not central planning is a workable system.

C. Only source 2 looks at this problem, and the others do not deal with it.

D. Only source 4 looks at this situation. The other sources do not deal with it.

49. D

A. Source 1 condemns the inefficiency and low living standards of the Soviet Union.

B. Source 3 outlines the successes of central planning, but makes no mention of its use during emergencies.

C. Source 4 points out the usefulness of central planning, but also makes no mention of its use in emergencies.

D. The example in source 5 of central planning during times of war clearly shows the usefulness of central planning during emergencies.

50. A

A. Source 1 states that "... the more talented Soviet citizens escaped from the country..."

B. Source 2 is critical of central planning, but does not mention the defection of any of its citizens.

C. Source 3 is not critical of the central planning.

D. Source 5 is not critical of central planning.

51. B

A. Source 2 is entirely critical of central planning. It makes no mention of any successes.

B. Source 3 mentions many of the successes of central planning, especially in the areas of social services.

C. Source 4 focuses on the use of central planning in all societies.

D. Source 5 focuses on the use of central planing in emergency situations.

52. A

A. Source 2 condemns central planning and suggests that modern economies are too complicated to plan.

B. Source 3 praises central planning and makes no mention of its failures.

C. Source 4 points out the advantages of central planning even in capitalist economies.

D. Source 5 points out the uses of central planning in times of war.

53. D

A. Source 1 makes no mention of services intended for use by the entire population.

B. Source 2 focuses on the weakness of central planning, not on its virtues.

C. Source 3 points out the successes of central planning without focusing on facilities that are intended to benefit everyone.

D. Source 4 illustrates the strengths of central planning by using the creation of public facilities as examples.

54. C

A. It is unlikely that the full employment policy saved the government much money due to the low level of productivity that resulted from it.

B. Although the Soviet Union liked to boast about its full employment, this was not the major reason for the full employment policy.

C. In the Soviet Union, a job was considered a right. Therefore, all Soviet citizens had to be provided jobs even if many of the jobs provided were not very useful.

D. Soviet industry could have had a reliable workforce without having full employment.

55. D

A. The level of training of Soviet workers was not as great a problem as the lack of initiative in the Soviet system.

B. Although the Soviet economy was overly complex, this was not due to the full employment policy.

C. Although many Soviet workers were not happy with the Soviet economic system, there is little evidence to indicate that the lack of productivity in the Soviet Union was due to this attitude.

D. Soviet workers who did work hard were not rewarded any better than those who did not. This lack of incentive to perform well was a serious problem for the Soviet economy.

56. D

A. The effect of hoarding on job security would be almost non-existent.

B. The poor quality of Soviet goods did not influence hoarding nearly as much as the shortage of goods did.

C. Basic needs on the Soviet Union, such as food, clothing, and shelter, were usually well looked after.

D. The lack of response to consumer demand in the Soviet Union stimulated people to buy as much of certain products as they could get their hands on whenever they were available.

57. B

A. Job security would unlikely be affected by hoarding.

B. All Soviet citizens were supposed to have equal access to goods when they were available. Hoarding seriously harmed this principle.

C. Although this issue is related to hoarding, it was not the most serious factor in making it illegal.

D. This is an important principle of communism, but it is not related to the issue of hoarding.

58. A

A. Running any business at a loss is certainly an indication of the lack of a profit motive.

B. Demand for public transport in the Soviet Union was high, and supply was maintained to meet it.

C. Although there was no competition in most of the services provided in the Soviet Union, the most important principle being ignored in the example was the profit motive.

D. Although private ownership in the Soviet Union was extremely limited, it was not a factor in the provision of transport services in the Soviet Union.

59. D

A. The rate of inflation in the Soviet Union was not considered an important factor in the provision of social services.

B. Although this might be an important consideration, low cost transport in the Soviet Union was provided as a basic necessity.

C. A supporter of the Soviet system would not be likely to justify the low level of wages in the Soviet Union.

D. Soviet planners considered the cheap transportation to be a basic need of society.

60. A

A. The levels of ownership of consumer goods in Brazil and the Soviet Union are relatively close.

B. The information does deal with consumer goods but does not indicate that economic priorities were focused on consumer goods.

C. There is not enough information in the data to determine whether this statement is true or not.

D. There is not enough information in the data to determine whether this statement is true or not.

61. D

A. The information indicates that Canada was the country least willing to spend money on defence.

B. Defence spending in Britain did not match that of the Soviet Union as a percent of GNP.

C. Although high, American defence spending as a percent of GNP was less than that of the Soviet Union.

D. Clearly, the Soviet Union led all nations in the chart in military spending as a percent of GNP.

QUALITY OF LIFE

62. C

A. There is no mention of the mixed economy in any of the sources.

B. Only one of the sources mentions anything about workers.

C. There is considerable disagreement among the sources about whether or not central planning achieved what it was supposed to achieve – namely, an almost perfect society where all people were equal.

D. Only one of the sources mentions anything about advancement.

63. D

A. Source 1 focuses on the dreariness and lack of freedom of central planning.

B. Source 2 focuses on the social benefits provided by central planning.

C. Source 3 focuses on the economic restrictions of central planning.

D. Source 4 focuses on the equality of citizens in a centrally planned society.

64. A

A. Sources 1 and 3 list a number of restrictions on personal freedom in a centrally planned society.

B. Sources 2 and 4 list only the positive side of central planning.

C. Sources 4 and 5 are in disagreement over the merits of central planning. As a result, this is not the best answer.

D. Source 1 comments on the lack of freedoms under central planning, but source 5 focuses more on the unfairness of the system that existed in the Soviet Union.

65. D

A. Source 2 makes only positive statements about central planning.

B. Source 3 is critical of central planning, but does not deal with the issue of inequality.

C. Source 4 makes only positive statements about central planning.

D. Source 5 points out that true equality did not exist in the Soviet Union, as senior government officials acted like an unofficial upper class.

66. B

A. Source 1 makes no mention of security in a centrally planned system.

B. Source 2 lists a number of benefits that were available under central planning. These benefits would lead to a clear sense of security.

C. Source 4 describes several benefits of central planning, but does not emphasize security as much as source 2 does.

D. Source 5 is quite critical of central planning.

ANSWERS AND SOLUTIONS
ECONOMIC GROWTH: CANADA

1.	B	14.	C	27.	D	40.	A	53.	C
2.	B	15.	A	28.	D	41.	C	54.	C
3.	D	16.	B	29.	D	42.	D	55.	C
4.	B	17.	D	30.	D	43.	A	56.	B
5.	A	18.	C	31.	A	44.	B	57.	D
6.	A	19.	A	32.	B	45.	C		
7.	A	20.	D	33.	D	46.	D		
8.	D	21.	A	34.	A	47.	D		
9.	A	22.	B	35.	B	48.	B		
10.	B	23.	C	36.	A	49.	A		
11.	C	24.	B	37.	B	50.	B		
12.	A	25.	B	38.	B	51.	B		
13.	A	26.	B	39.	A	52.	D		

HOW TECHNOLOGICAL CHANGES HAVE AFFECTED OUR WAY OF LIFE

1. B

A. Source 1 depicts oil – a primary industry. But source 2 depicts a steel mill – a secondary industry.

B. Sources 1 and 3 both depict extractive industries based on natural resources, so they are primary industries.

C. Source 2 depicts a secondary industry and source 4 depicts a tertiary industry.

D. Sources 4 and 5 are both tertiary industries.

2. B

A. Source 1 depicts a primary industry.

B. Source 2 depicts a secondary industry. The manufacture of any item is a secondary industry.

C. Source 3 depicts a primary industry.

D. Source 4 depicts a tertiary industry. Any service is a tertiary industry.

3. D

A. Source 1 depicts oil – a primary industry. Source 2 depicts a steel mill – a secondary industry.

B. Source 2 depicts a secondary industry and source 3 depicts a primary industry.

C. Source 3 depicts a primary industry and source 4 is a tertiary industry.

D. Sources 4 and 5 both depict service industries which are tertiary industries.

4. B

A. Although several of the sources show the disruptive affects of change, it is not common to all of the sources.

B. Each scenario depicts a situation in which some part of society attempts to resist change.

C. While this statement is true, it is not depicted in most of the scenarios.

D. None of the scenarios depicts a situation that is harmful to all of society.

5. A

A. There is a parallel between the damaging of punch cards and the use of human tellers. In each case, people refuse to be served by machines.

B. Although there is a similarity, the deactivating of airbags is an act that endangers the user, as opposed to simply refusing to be served by a machine.

C. This is a matter of personal preference. It is not an example of refusing to use a certain technology.

D. Once again, this is a matter of personal choice. Whether rational or not, it is not harmful to the person making the choice.

6. A

A. In all of the scenarios it is shown that resistance to technological change has been unsuccessful.

B. Although this is true of some of the technologies in the scenarios, it is not true of all of them.

C. The history of technological change shows that this statement is usually incorrect.

D. Attempts to prevent technological change through violence have always failed.

7. A

A. Scenarios 1 and 2 are the best choice for this question. Both scenarios depict violent attempts to halt technological change.

B. Scenario 3 lacks the aspect of violence that accompanies scenario 2.

C. Neither scenario depicts any appreciable level of violent opposition to change.

D. Neither scenario depicts any appreciable level of violent opposition to change.

8. D

A. The source does indicate that the predictions made are not based on fact, but rather that such predictions might be overly speculative.

B. There is no indication that the predictions discussed were realistic.

C. Personal biases enter into all predictions to some extent, but this is not the main idea of the source.

D. The main idea of the source is that predictions about technology are often not accurate.

9. A

A. The source indicates that people and institutions are often slow to take advantage of new technology. This is often due to the fact that existing institutions are set up in such a way that new developments are not accommodated very well.

B. There is nothing in the source to indicate that the technologies mentioned have not played a major role in human development.

C. Although this is often true, there is nothing in the source dealing with this aspect of technology.

D. While this is also true, it is not the main point of the source.

10. B

A. The word *thrifty* in the cartoon is misleading. Saving money is not the point of the cartoon.

B. The humour in the cartoon stems from the fact that the customer in the cartoon does not understand modern computer technology.

C. What is suggested in the cartoon is not just difficult, it is impossible.

D. No special use is suggested for computers that would actually work.

11. C

A. The term *mechanization* refers to the replacement of human labour by machines.

B. The term *automation* refers to the replacement of machines run by people with machines that run themselves.

C. The term *cybernation* refers to the replacement of machines that are supervised by people to machines that are supervised by other machines – namely computers.

D. The term *industrialization* refers to the entire process of going from a society that uses mainly human and animal labour to a society based on machines and industry.

12. A

A. Persons opposed to job losses created by machines have frequently advocated that replacement of people by machines be either slowed down or halted.

B. Retraining workers would not stop the original job losses.

C. Modernization of government would create further job losses.

D. Efficiency would decline if technological improvements were halted.

13. A

A. The quality of being human is one area in which machines cannot compete well yet.

B. This is true for certain jobs, but so far technological change has created more jobs than it has replaced.

C. Only in the most specialized and artistic tasks can humans outperform machines.

D. This may be true, but it will still occur if it saves money in the long term.

14. C

A. This may be true, but it is not really a recommendation for technological change.

B. Most people would not accept this as much of a benefit.

C. This is the best answer. Technology can only be sold if it benefits society.

D. Most people believe that companies make enough profit without taking away jobs.

15. A

A. The main issue is whether or not technological change is really necessary, and whether or not the things that it brings are of any real value.

B. None of the sources deals with the causes of technological change.

C. None of the sources attempts to evaluate technological change from the point of view of whether or not it is important.

D. This is certainly stressed by source 5, but the other sources do not emphasize it.

16. B

A. Source 1 and 2 definitely stress that dramatic change is usually emphasized, but source 3 focuses on the attempts to popularize change.

B. Sources 1, 2, and 4 all indicate that change is sometimes overly sensationalized. Source 4 emphasizes that most changes are not sensational in nature, but modest and useful.

C. Only source 4 focuses on the sensational nature of certain types of change.

D. Source 3 does not deal with the emphasis on sensationalism of change.

17. D

A. Sources 1 and 2 definitely do not oppose change.

B. Source 3 opposes change, but source 2 does not.

C. Source 4 strongly supports certain types of change.

D. Source 3 points out that progress has created considerable harm. Source 5 gives examples of what it considers dangerous or useless products.

18. C

A. Source 3 does not go so far as to state that there is a conspiracy to promote change, but indicates that there is a good deal of pressure applied to those members of society who oppose it.

B. This may well be true, but it is not the point that source 3 is trying to make.

C. This is the main idea behind source 3. People are often convinced to accept change simply because much change has positive connotations.

D. Most people are aware of changes, especially when they bother to reminisce about the past.

19. A

A. The development of the motion picture industry is a good example of a profound change that has been of great benefit to society, without creating much harm.

B. The source does not make this claim, even though it is usually true.

C. Source 4 would probably make this claim, but it is not the main point of the information given.

D. Source 4 clearly believes that the motion picture industry has had a major impact on society.

THE MIXED ECONOMY

20. D

A. Source 1 is typical of what happened to many workers during the economic reforms that took place in the former Soviet Union. Source 2 is typical of a market economy, but Source 1 is not.

B. Source 2 is typical of a market economy, but source 3 is not.

C. Neither source is typical of a market economy.

D. Both sources are typical of a market economy, in which workers are expected to fend for themselves in the workplace.

21. A

A. Under *perestroika*, Soviet businesses were required to become more efficient. As a result, many workers who once had jobs for life found themselves looking for work.

B. Source 2 is typical of a market economy.

C. Source 3 is typical of a socialist mixed economy.

D. Source 4 is typical of a market economy.

22. B

A. Source 1 depicts the changes that occurred in the Soviet Union under *perestroika*.

B. Source 2 depicts a market economy, during one of the periodic slowdowns that occur under that economic system.

C. Source 3 is typical of a socialist mixed economy.

D. Source 4 is typical of a market economy, but in this case there is no hint that the economy is slowing down. In a market economy, there is always a certain level of unemployment.

23. C

A. Source 1 is typical of what occurred in the Soviet Union under Mikhail Gorbachev.

B. Source 2 is typical of a market economy.

C. Source 3 is typical of a socialist mixed economy such as Sweden's. In these societies, it is considered the responsibility of the state to retrain workers who have lost their jobs.

D. Source 4 is typical of a market economy.

24. B

A. Although two of the scenarios address dealing with pollution, scenarios 1 and 2 do not.

B. All of the scenarios deal with the problem of pollution and its consequences.

C. Only scenario 2 deals with the human cost of pollution.

D. Only scenario 3 deals with penalties for those who pollute.

25. B

A. Scenario 1 is most typical of a market economy with some environmental regulation.

B. In the Soviet Union, the lack of political freedoms made it difficult to do anything about mistakes made by the central government. As a result, damage to the environment was widespread and Soviet citizens were victimized by their own government.

C. Scenario 3 is typical of a market or mixed economy with strict environmental regulations.

D. Scenario 4 is typical of a market economy.

26. B

A. Scenario 2 certainly indicates problems from a lack of enforcement, but scenario 4 does not.

B. Scenarios 1, 2, and 3 also indicate that strict enforcement of environmental laws is needed to encourage businesses to operate in an environmentally friendly manner.

C. Scenarios 2 and 3 indicate the importance of the enforcement of environmental laws, but source 4 does not.

D. Scenario 1 indicates the problems of a lack of enforcement, but source 4 does not.

27. D

A. Scenario 1 seems to indicate that cheating on environmental standards is a way to save money.

B. Scenario 2 does not mention the economic impact of damaging the environment.

C. Scenario 3 focuses only on the enforcement of environmental standards.

D. Scenario 4 shows that businesses can actually save money by polluting less. This is a lesson that many Canadian and American businesses have learned in recent years. In addition, companies that pollute less improve their images in the eyes of the consumers.

28. D

A. Scenario 1 certainly indicates this, but scenario 2 does not.

B. Although scenario 3 deals with the enforcement of environmental laws, scenario 2 focuses on the human impact of environmental damage, but not on criminal penalties.

C. Scenario 3 deals with the enforcement of environmental laws, but scenario 4 does not.

D. Both scenarios 1 and 3 indicate that strict enforcement of environmental standards is required to encourage businesses to clean up their acts.

29. D

A. Source 1 is typical of a centrally planned economy.

B. Source 2 could be any of several different types of economic systems.

C. Source 3 is typical of a market economy.

D. Source 4 indicates that drug prices are partially controlled, which is typical of certain mixed economies, including Sweden, Norway, Denmark, and other western European nations.

30. D

A. Source 1 is typical of a centrally planned economy.

B. Source 2 could be any of several different types of economic systems.

C. Source 3 is typical of a market economy.

D. Source 5 depicts a traditional economy, a system in which producers consume most of what they produce themselves, and then sell whatever they have left over to buy a few necessities. In such a society, consumer demand is usually low.

31. A

A. Under central planning, shortages of consumer goods were common and often led to scenes like the one described.

B. Source 3 is typical of a market economy.

C. Source 4 is typical of a mixed economy.

D. Source 5 is typical of a traditional economy.

32. B

A. Source 1 is typical of a centrally planned economy.

B. Source 3 depicts a situation that often occurs in the boom and bust cycle of the market economy. Frequently, consumer demand outstrips available supply, forcing prices to rise until the supply catches up to the demand.

C. Source 4 is typical of a mixed economy.

D. Source 5 is typical of a traditional economy.

33. D

A. Source 2 depicts a market or mixed or even a centrally planned economy, in which such things as garage sales are common. Under these systems, most goods are produced for consumption by someone other than the producer.

B. Source 3 is a market economy. Under this system, most goods are produced to be sold to someone other than the producer.

C. Source 4 depicts a mixed economy. In this system, most goods are produced for consumption by persons other than the producer.

D. Source 5 depicts a traditional economy. Under this system, the level of production is so low that most goods produced are consumed by the producer, as there is little left to sell.

34. A

A. The limousine represents a strong economy. The people labeled "poor" represent those parts of the population that economic success has left behind.

B. There is no indication that the cartoonist considers members of the poor to be lazy.

C. There is no indication that the cartoonist is attempting to comment on the purchasing power of the poor.

D. While this is shown in the cartoon, it is not the point the cartoonist is trying to get across.

35. B

A. Lowering interest rates would help to speed up the economy, but decreasing government spending would slow it down.

B. Increasing taxes on the wealthy would provide funds to increase spending on social services to help the poorest members of society.

C. This is an extreme measure, and would be more typical of a person who favours a centrally planned economy.

D. Lowering taxes on all parts of the population might help the poor, but it would be of little use to those persons who do not have jobs.

36. A

A. Increasing government control over the economy would theoretically enable the government to share the wealth of society more evenly.

B. Slowing down the economy would make the situation worse for all segments of society.

C. Creation of work camps would be regarded as a desperate measure and not a permanent solution to the problem of unemployment and poverty.

D. Reducing welfare benefits would be unlikely to force people back to work if there are no jobs to be found. Also, a supporter of central planning would be likely to sympathize with the poor and would be, therefore, unlikely to remove any of their privileges.

37. B

A. A real capitalist might do this, but interestingly many advocates of the market system see nothing wrong with accepting government help when it is offered.

B. Reducing taxes on the wealthy might further stimulate the economy and create more jobs.

C. Reducing the number of days required to qualify for unemployment benefits would provide swifter economic relief for the newly unemployed, but it might have little effect if there are no jobs available in the first place.

D. Reduction of government orders to private industry would slow down the economy and create more unemployment.

38. B

A. There is no way of determining the rate of economic growth from the information given.

B. A mixed economy attempts to combine the strongest features of central planning and the market system. As a result, citizens in a mixed economy are provided with many benefits and the economy is more strongly regulated than in a market system.

C. Although economic freedom is important in a mixed economy, the market system is closely supervised by the government.

D. There is more government control in a market economy and more social security.

39. A

A. Most supporters of a market economy consider mixed economies to be over-regulated.

B. Most supporters of a market system are opposed to poverty, however, they usually believe that government regulation cannot solve this problem.

C. More industrial infrastructure would be supported by any economic system.

D. Schools and other social services are usually considered appropriate areas for government action even by those who support the market system.

40. A

- **A. Supporters of the mixed economy place the highest value on promotion of economic and social equality.**
- B. Suggesting that opponents of a mixed economy leave the country would be considered most undemocratic by supporters of a mixed economy.
- C. Selfishness might be suggested as a motive of their opponents, but would not be as important as the goal of economic and social equality.
- D. Most social democrats (those who support a mixed economy) would not be too concerned about benefitting the rich.

41. C

- A. Increasing taxes and raising interest rates would create even more unemployment by slowing down the economy even more.
- B. Reducing government spending would reduce the rate of economic growth and make unemployment worse.
- **C. Increasing spending on social programs and public works would stimulate the economy and create more jobs.**
- D. Reducing taxes on foreign goods would increase foreign competition and result in more job losses.

42. D

- A. This might be true, but it is hard to determine the exact effect of social programs on the crime rate.
- B. Very few supporters of social services would go so far as to claim the support of "the Lord."
- C. Giving those who do not pay taxes government services would be a weak argument in favour of social services.
- **D. Promoting equality and helping those in need are important to any supporter of a mixed economy.**

QUALITY OF LIFE

43. A

- **A. Increasing spending on social services would be expected to provide the poor with the services that they need until they are capable of looking after themselves.**
- B. Reducing employment insurance might force people to look more actively for jobs, but would not necessarily lower the rate of poverty.
- C. Increasing grants to private businesses might stimulate the economy, but again would not necessarily eliminate poverty. This would be especially true concerning members of society who cannot work due to illness or old age.
- D. Encouraging students to stay in school longer would increase the students' chances of finding employment once they graduate, but it would do little to help those who were already living in poverty.

44. B

A. High levels of government spending might be the reason for the decline in value of the currency in the first place. Increasing such spending would probably only make matters worse.

B. Increasing interest rates would encourage citizens to invest in their own economy and would also encourage foreigners to invest in the economy as well. This would create a demand for the currency of the country in question and increase its value.

C. Printing more money would make the value of the currency decline even more. If enough money was printed, it might destroy the value of the currency completely, as happened in Germany in the 1920s.

D. Reducing government spending might prop up the value of the currency, but not as quickly as raising interest rates.

45. C

A. Most nations maintain some sort of military regardless of their economic ideals.

B. Publicly funded fire departments are characteristic of all economic systems. It is considered a basic function of government.

C. Societies can choose to either have a public school system paid for by taxes or a private system paid for by those who receive the education. Public school systems are characteristic of a mixed economy.

D. Maintenance of navigational aids is considered a basic function of government in all economic systems.

46. D

A. Supporters of central planning and supporters of mixed economies usually support the goal of achieving economic equality even though this goal is not as strongly emphasized in a mixed economy.

B. Although government involvement in a centrally planned economy is greater than it is in a mixed economy, the level of government ownership would not be the most serious source of disagreement.

C. Both centrally planned and mixed economies have a certain level of government planning. It is, however, less in a mixed economy. Again this would not be a area of serious disagreement.

D. Mixed economies are considered social democracies by their supporters and are characterized by very high levels of political freedoms. A supporter of a mixed economy would disagree with a supporter of central planning most strongly in this area.

47. D

A. Both mixed economies and market economies attempt to supply their citizens with consumer goods.

B. Both mixed economies and market economies promote high levels of competition between private businesses.

C. Both mixed economies and market economies attempt to create as much wealth as possible for their citizens.

D. Supporters of mixed economies find the concentration of wealth in the hands of a few very wealthy people and the large number of poor people in a market economy to be unacceptable.

48. B

A. None of the sources is concerned about stimulating the economy.

B. The main source of disagreement between the sources is whether or not government should involve itself in the regulation of a market economy.

C. Source 1 is definitely not concerned about the welfare of workers.

D. None of the sources are in disagreement about the system that best creates wealth.

49. A

A. Source 1 accuses government of frustrating business with "...a tangle of government regulations... ."

B. Source 2 believes that government regulation is necessary to protect the environment and the worker.

C. Source 3 believes government regulation is necessary to protect the consumer.

D. Source 4 believes government regulation is necessary to provide adequate safeguards to society.

50. B

A. This answer is contradicted by source 1, 2, and 4.

B. Sources 2, 3, and 4 all claim that government regulation will protect the public in some way.

C. None of the sources is in favour of reducing the levels of profit of the business community.

D. Only source 4 claims that government regulation will promote equality.

51. B

A. Source 1 does not support the mixed economy in any way.

B. Source 2 is concerned about "...serious damage to the environment."

C. Source 3 does not mention environmental concerns.

D. Source 4 also does not mention environmental concerns.

52. D

A. Source 1 believes that the mixed economy slows down the market system.

B. Source 2 does not emphasize the idea of sharing the wealth of society.

C. Source 3 is most concerned about protecting the consumer.

D. Source 4 states the "...average citizen would share in the wealth... ."

53. C

A. Regulation of wages and prices is more characteristic of central planning.

B. Allowing supply and demand to determine wages and prices is characteristic of a market economy.

C. Minimum wage laws are characteristic of a mixed economy.

D. Complete regulation of labour and wages is characteristic of central planning.

54. C

A. The term "market" indicates that this action is typical of a market economy.

B. Allowing the government to determine what goods and services will be provided is a characteristic of central planning.

C. In a mixed economy, the government provides what are considered to be essential services, such as schools and hospitals, and the private sector provides the rest.

D. Only in a centrally planned system would the government provide all goods and services.

55. C

A. Pharmaceutical supplies would be provided to the consumer by private businesses such as the local drug store.

B. Automobiles would be provided to the consumer by privately owned dealerships such as those that exist in Canada.

C. Public schools, as the name implies, are considered a government service in most mixed economies.

D. Security guards are private police forces whose services are contracted out.

56. B

A. Complete lack of regulation regarding goods and services is characteristic of an unregulated market economy.

B. In countries with mixed economies, such as Canada, there are numerous government regulations to ensure that consumers do not encounter dangerous or poorly made products.

C. Requiring consumers to determine the quality of goods and services themselves is characteristic of a complete market economy.

D. Manufacture of consumer goods is characteristic of a centrally planned economy.

57. D

A. Privatization of government owned business is not likely to reduce levels of unemployment.

B. This might create a few more jobs if the businesses were run less efficiently, but it is not a good long or short-term solution.

C. Reducing government spending would increase the level of unemployment.

D. Reducing taxes would give the average consumer more spending power and stimulate the private sector, thus creating more jobs.

NOTES

KEY STRATEGIES FOR SUCCESS ON EXAMS

KEY STRATEGIES FOR SUCCESS ON EXAMS

There are many different ways to assess your knowledge and understanding of course concepts. Depending on the subject, your knowledge and skills are most often assessed through a combination of methods which may include performances, demonstrations, projects, products, and oral and written tests. Written exams are one of the most common methods currently used in schools. Just as there are some study strategies that help you to improve your academic performance, there are also some test writing strategies that may help you to do better on unit test and year-end exams. To do your best on any test, you need to be well prepared. You must know the course content and be as familiar as possible with the manner in which it is usually tested. Applying test writing strategies may help you to become more successful on exams, improve your grades, and achieve your potential.

STUDY OPTIONS FOR EXAM PREPARATION

Studying and preparing for exams requires a strong sense of self-discipline. Sometimes having a study buddy or joining a study group

- helps you to stick to your study schedule
- ensures you have others with whom you can practice making and answering sample questions
- clarifies information and provides peer support

It may be helpful to use a combination of individual study, working with a study buddy, or joining a study group to prepare for your unit test or year-end exam. Be sure that the study buddy or group you choose to work with is positive, knowledgeable, motivated, and supportive. Working with a study buddy or a study group usually means you have to begin your exam preparation earlier than you would if you are studying independently.

Tutorial classes are often helpful in preparing for exams. You can ask a knowledgeable student to tutor you or you can hire a private tutor. Sometimes school jurisdictions or individual schools may offer tutorials and study sessions to assist students in preparing for exams. Tutorial services are also offered by companies that specialize in preparing students for exams. Information regarding tutorial services is usually available from school counsellors, local telephone directories, and on-line search engines.

EXAM QUESTION FORMATS

There is no substitute for knowing the course content. To do well in your course you need to combine your subject knowledge and understanding with effective test writing skills. Being familiar with question formats may help you in preparing for quizzes, unit tests or year-end exams. The most typical question formats include multiple choice, numerical response, written response, and essay. The following provides a brief description of each format and suggestions for how you might consider responding to each of the formats.

MULTIPLE CHOICE

A multiple choice question provides some information for you to consider and then requires you to select a response from four choices, often referred to as distracters. The distracters may complete a statement, be a logical extension or application of the information. In preparing for multiple choice questions you may wish to focus on:

- studying concepts, theories, groups of facts or ideas that are similar in meaning; **compare and contrast their similarities and differences**; ask yourself "How do the concepts differ?", "Why is the difference important?", "What does each fact or concept mean or include?" "What are the exceptions?"
- **identifying main ideas, key information**, formulas, concepts, and theories, where they apply and what the **exceptions** are
- memorizing important definitions, examples, and applications of key concepts
- learning to **recognize *distracters*** that may lead you to apply plausible but incorrect solutions, and ***three and one splits*** where one answer is obviously incorrect and the others are very similar in meaning or wording
- **using active reading techniques** such as underlining, highlighting, numbering, and circling important facts, dates, basic points
- making up your own multiple choice questions for practice

Numerical Response

A numerical response question provides information and requires you to use a calculation to arrive at the response. In preparing for numerical response questions you may wish to focus on:

- memorizing formulas and their applications
- completing chapter questions or making up your own for practice
- making a habit of **estimating the answer** prior to completing the calculation
- paying special **attention to accuracy** in computing and the use of significant digits where applicable

Written Response

A written response question requires you to respond to a question or directive such as "explain", "compare", contrast". In preparing for written response questions you may wish to focus on:

- ensuring your response **answers the question**
- recognizing **directing words** such as "list", "explain", "define"
- providing **concise answers** within the time limit you are devoting to the written response section of the exam
- identifying subject content that lends itself to short answer questions

Essay

An essay is a lengthier written response requiring you to identify your position on an issue and provide logical thinking or evidence that supports the basis of your argument. In preparing for an essay you may wish to focus on:

- examining **issues** that are relevant or related to the subject area or **application of the concept**
- comparing and contrasting two points of view, articles, or theories
- considering the merits of the opposite point of view
- identifying **key concepts**, principles or ideas
- providing **evidence**, examples, and **supporting information** for your viewpoint
- preparing two or three essays on probable topics
- **writing an outline** and essay within the defined period of time you will have for the exam
- understanding the "marker's expectations"

KEY TIPS FOR ANSWERING COMMON EXAM QUESTION FORMATS

Most exams use a variety of question formats to test your understanding. You must provide responses to questions ranging from lower level, information recall types to higher level, critical thinking types. The following information provides you with some suggestions on how to prepare for answering multiple choice, written response and essay questions.

MULTIPLE CHOICE

Multiple choice questions often require you to make fine distinctions between correct and nearly correct answers so it is imperative that you:

- begin by answering only the questions for which you are certain of the correct answer
- read the question stem and formulate your own response before you read the choices available
- read the directions carefully paying close attention to words such as "mark ***all*** correct", "choose the ***most*** correct" and "choose the ***one best*** answer"
- use active reading techniques such as underlining, circling, or highlighting critical words and phrases
- watch for superlatives such as "all", "every", "none", "always" which indicate that the correct response must be an undisputed fact
- watch for negatives such as "none", "never", "neither", "not" which indicate that the correct response must be an undisputed fact
- examine all of the alternatives in questions which include "all of the above" or "none of the above" as responses to ensure that "all" or "none" of the statements apply *totally*
- be aware of distracters that may lead you to apply plausible but incorrect solutions, and 'three and one splits' where one answer is obviously incorrect and the others are very similar in meaning or wording
- use information from other questions to help you
- eliminate the responses you know are wrong and then assess the remaining alternatives and choose the best one
- guess if you are not certain

Written Response

Written response questions usually require a very specific answer. In answering these questions you should:

- underline key words or phrases that indicate what is required in your answer such as "three reasons", "list", or "give an example"
- write down rough, point-form notes regarding the information you want to include in your answer
- be brief and only answer what is asked
- reread your response to ensure you have answered the question
- use the appropriate subject vocabulary and terminology in your response
- use point form to complete as many questions as possible if you are running out of time

Essay

Essay questions often give you the opportunity to demonstrate the breadth and depth of your learning regarding a given topic. In responding to these questions it may be helpful to:

- read the question carefully and underline key words and phrases
- make a brief outline to organize the flow of the information and ideas you want to include in your response
- ensure you have an introduction, body, and conclusion
- begin with a clear statement of your view, position, or interpretation of the question
- address only one main point or key idea in each paragraph and include relevant supporting information and examples
- assume the reader has no prior knowledge of your topic
- conclude with a strong summary statement
- use appropriate subject vocabulary and terminology when and where it is applicable
- review your essay for clarity of thought, logic, grammar, punctuation, and spelling
- write as legibly as you can
- double space your work in case you need to edit it when you proof read your essay
- complete the essay in point form if you run short of time

KEY Tips for Responding to Common 'Directing' Words

There are some commonly used words in exam questions that require you to respond in a predetermined or expected manner. The following provides you with a brief summary of how you may wish to plan your response to exam questions that contain these words.

- **Evaluate** (to assess the worth of something)
  - Determine the use, goal, or ideal from which you can judge something's worth
  - Make a value judgment or judgments on something
  - Make a list of reasons for the judgment
  - Develop examples, evidence, contrasts, and details to support your judgments and clarify your reasoning

- **Discuss** (usually to give pros and cons regarding an assertion, quotation, or policy)
  - Make a list of bases for comparing and contrasting
  - Develop details and examples to support or clarify each pro and con
  - On the basis of your lists, conclude your response by stating the extent to which you agree or disagree with what is asserted

- **Compare and Contrast** (to give similarities and differences of two or more objects, beliefs, or positions)
  - Make a list of bases for comparing and contrasting
  - For each basis, judge similarities and differences
  - Supply details, evidence, and examples that support and clarify your judgment
  - Assess the overall similarity or difference
  - Determine the significance of similarity or difference in connection with the purpose of the comparison

- **Analyze** (to break into parts)
  - Break the topic, process, procedure, or object of the essay into its major parts
  - Connect and write about the parts according to the direction of the question: describe, explain, criticize

- **Criticize** (to judge strong and weak points of something)
  - Make a list of the strong points and weak points

- Develop details, examples, and contrasts to support judgments
- Make an overall judgment of quality

- **EXPLAIN** (to show causes of or reasons for something)
  - In Science, usually show the process that occurs in moving from one state or phase in a process to the next, thoroughly presenting details of each step
  - In Humanities and often in Social Sciences, make a list of factors that influence something, developing evidence for each factor's potential influence

- **DESCRIBE** (to give major features of something)
  - Pick out highlights or major aspects of something
  - Develop details and illustrations to give a clear picture

- **ARGUE** (to give reasons for one position and against another)
  - Make a list of reasons for the position
  - Make a list of reasons against the position
  - Refute objections to your reasons for and defend against objections to your reasons opposing the position
  - Fill out reasons, objections, and replies with details, examples, consequences, and logical connections

- **COMMENT** (to make statements about something)
  - Calls for a position, discussion, explanation, judgment, or evaluation regarding a subject, idea, or situation
  - Is strengthened by providing supporting evidence, information, and examples

- **DEMONSTRATE** (to show something)
  - Depending upon the nature of the subject matter, provide evidence, clarify the logical basis of something, appeal to principles or laws as in an explanation, supply a range of opinion and examples

- **SYNTHESIZE** (to invent a new or different version)
  - Construct your own meaning based upon your knowledge and experiences
  - Support your assertion with examples, references to literature and research studies

(Source: http://www.counc.ivic.ca/learn/program/hndouts/simple.html)

TEST ANXIETY

Do you get test anxiety? Most students feel some level of stress, worry, or anxiety before an exam. Feeling a little tension or anxiety before or during an exam is normal for most students. A little stress or tension may help you rise to the challenge but too much stress or anxiety interferes with your ability to do well on the exam. Test anxiety may cause you to experience some of the following in a mild or more severe form:

- "butterflies" in your stomach, sweating, shortness of breath, or a quickened pulse
- disturbed sleep or eating patterns
- increased nervousness, fear, or irritability
- sense of hopelessness or panic
- drawing a "blank" during the exam

If you experience extreme forms of test anxiety you need to consult your family physician. For milder forms of anxiety you may find some of the following strategies effective in helping you to remain calm and focused during your unit tests or year-end exams.

- Acknowledge that you are feeling some stress or test anxiety and that this is normal
- Focus upon your breathing, taking several deep breaths
- Concentrate upon a single object for a few moments
- Tense and relax the muscles in areas of your body where you feel tension
- Break your exam into smaller, manageable, achievable parts
- Use positive self-talk to calm and motivate yourself. Tell yourself, "I can do this if I read carefully/start with the easy questions/focus on what I know/stick with it/. . ." instead of saying, "I can't do this."
- Visualize your successful completion of your review or the exam
- Recall a time in the past when you felt calm, relaxed, and content. Replay this experience in your mind experiencing it as fully as possible.

KEY STRATEGIES FOR SUCCESS BEFORE AN EXAM – A CHECKLIST

Review, review, review. That's a huge part of your exam preparation. Here's a quick review checklist for you to see how many strategies for success you are using as you prepare to write your unit tests and year-end exams.

KEY Strategies for Success Before an Exam	*Yes*	*No*
Have you been attending classes?		
Have you determined your learning style?		
Have you organized a quiet study area for yourself?		
Have you developed a long-term study schedule?		
Have you developed a short-term study schedule?		
Are you working with a study buddy or study group?		
Is your study buddy/group positive, knowledgeable, motivated and supportive?		
Have you registered in tutorial classes?		
Have you developed your exam study notes?		
Have you reviewed previously administered exams?		
Have you practiced answering multiple choice, numerical response, written response, and essay questions?		
Have you analyzed the most common errors students make on each subject exam?		
Have you practiced strategies for controlling your exam anxiety?		
Have you maintained a healthy diet and sleep routine?		
Have you participated in regular physical activity?		

KEY STRATEGIES FOR SUCCESS DURING AN EXAM

Doing well on any exam requires that you prepare in advance by reviewing your subject material and then using your knowledge to respond effectively to the exam questions during the test session. Combining subject knowledge with effective test writing skills gives you the best opportunity for success. The following are some strategies you may find useful in writing your exam.

- Managing Test Anxiety
  - Be as prepared as possible to increase your self-confidence.
  - Arrive at the exam on time and bring whatever materials you need to complete the exam such as pens, pencils, erasers, and calculators if they are allowed.
  - Drink enough water before you begin the exam so you are hydrated.
  - Associate with positive, calm individuals until you enter the exam room.
  - Use positive self-talk to calm yourself.
  - Remind yourself that it is normal to feel anxious about the exam.
  - Visualize your successful completion of the exam.
  - Breathe deeply several times.
  - Rotate your head, shrug your shoulders, and change positions to relax.

- While the information from your crib notes is still fresh in your memory, write down the key words, concepts, definitions, theories or formulas on the back of the test paper before you look at the exam questions.
  - Review the entire exam.
  - Budget your time.
  - Begin with the easiest question or the question that you know you can answer correctly rather than following the numerical question order of the exam.
  - Be aware of linked questions and use the clues to help you with other questions or in other parts of the exam.

If you "blank" on the exam, try repeating the deep breathing and physical relaxation activities first. Then move to visualization and positive self-talk to get you going. You can also try to open the 'information flow' by writing down anything that you remember about the subject on the reverse side of your exam paper. This activity sometimes helps you to remind yourself that you <u>do</u> know something and you are capable of writing the exam.

GETTING STARTED

Managing Your Time

- Plan on staying in the exam room for the full time that is available to you.
- Review the entire exam and calculate how much time you can spend on each section. Write your time schedule on the top of your paper and stick as closely as possible to the time you have allotted for each section of the exam.
- Be strategic and use your time where you will get the most marks. Avoid spending too much time on challenging questions that are not worth more marks than other questions that may be easier and are worth the same number of marks.
- If you are running short of time, switch to point form and write as much as you can for written response and essay questions so you have a chance of receiving partial marks.
- Leave time to review your paper asking yourself, "Did I do all of the questions I was supposed to do?", "Can I answer any questions now that I skipped over before?", "Are there any questions that I misinterpreted or misread?"

Using the Five Pass Method

- **Browsing Stage** – Scan the entire exam noting the format, the specific instructions and marks allotted for each section, which questions you will complete and which ones you will omit if there is a choice.
- **The First Answering Pass** – To gain confidence and momentum, answer only the questions you are confident you can answer correctly and quickly. These questions are most often found in the multiple choice or numerical response sections of the exam. Maintain a brisk pace; if a question is taking too long to answer, leave it for the Second or Third Pass.
- **The Second Answering Pass** – This Pass addresses questions which require more effort per mark. Answer as many of the remaining questions as possible while maintaining steady progress toward a solution. As soon as it becomes evident the question is too difficult or is tasking an inordinate amount of time, leave it for the Third Answering Pass.
- **The Third Answering Pass** – During the Third Answering Pass you should complete all partial solutions from the first two Passes. Marks are produced at a slower rate during this stage. At the end of this stage, all questions should have full or partial answers. Guess at any multiple choice questions that you have not yet answered.
- **The Final Review Stage** – Use the remaining time to review the entire exam, making sure that no questions have been overlooked. Check answers and calculations as time permits.

Using the Three Pass Method

- **Overview** – Begin with an overview of the exam to see what it contains. Look for 'easy' questions and questions on topics that you know thoroughly.
- **Second Pass** – Answer all the questions that you can complete without too much trouble. These questions help to build your confidence and establish a positive start.
- **Last Pass** – Now go through and answer the questions that are left. This is when you begin to try solving the questions you find particularly challenging.

KEY EXAM TIPS FOR SELECTED SUBJECT AREAS

The following are a few additional suggestions you may wish to consider when writing exams in any of the selected subject areas.

English Language Arts

Exams in English Language Arts usually have two components, writing and reading. Sometimes students are allowed to bring approved reference books such as a dictionary, thesaurus and writing handbook into the exam. If you have not used these references on a regular basis, you may find them more of a hindrance than a help in an exam situation. In completing the written section of an English Language Arts exam:

- plan your essay
- focus on the issue presented
- establish a clear position using a thesis statement to direct and unify your writing
- organize your writing in a manner that logically presents your views
- support your viewpoint with specific examples
- edit and proof read your writing

In completing the reading section of an English Language Arts exam:

- read the entire selection before responding
- use titles, dates, footnotes, pictures, introductions, and notes on the author to assist you in developing an understanding of the piece presented
- when using line references, read a few lines before and after the identified section

MATHEMATICS

In some instances, the use of calculators is permitted (or required) to complete complex calculations, modeling, simulations, or to demonstrate your use of technology. It is imperative that you are familiar with the approved calculator and the modes you may be using during your exam. In writing exams in mathematics:

- use appropriate mathematical notation and symbols
- clearly show or explain all the steps involved in solving the problem
- check to be sure you have included the correct units of measurement and have rounded to the appropriate significant digit
- use appropriate labelling and equal increments on graphs

SCIENCES

In the Sciences written response and open-ended questions usually require a clear, organized, and detailed explanation of the science involved in the question. You may find it helpful to use the acronym **STEEPLES** to organize your response to these types of questions. STEEPLES stands for **S**cience, **T**echnological, **E**cological, **E**thical, **P**olitical, **L**egal, **E**conomical, and **S**ocial aspects of the issue presented. In writing exams in the sciences:

- use scientific vocabulary to clearly explain your understanding of the processes or issues
- state your position in an objective manner
- demonstrate your understanding of both sides of the issue
- clearly label graphs, diagrams, tables, and charts using accepted conventions
- provide all formulas and equations

SOCIAL STUDIES, HISTORY, GEOGRAPHY

Exams in these courses of study often require you to take a position on an issue and defend your point of view. Your response should demonstrate your understanding of both the positive and negative aspects of the issue and be supported by well-considered arguments and evidence. In writing exams in Social Studies, History or Geography, the following acronyms may be helpful to you in organizing your approach.

- **SEE** – stands for **S**tatement, **E**xplanation, **E**xample. This acronym reminds you to couple your statement regarding your position with an explanation and then an example.

- **PERMS** – stands for **P**olitical, **E**conomic, **R**eligious or moral, **M**ilitary, and **S**ocietal values. Your position statement may be derived from or based upon any of these points of view. Your argument is more credible if you can show that recognized authorities such as leaders, theorists, writers or scientists back your position.

SUMMARY

Writing exams involves a certain amount of stress and anxiety. If you want to do your best on the exam, *there is no substitute for being well prepared.* Being well prepared helps you to feel more confident about your ability to succeed and less anxious about writing tests. In preparing for unit or year-end exams remember to:

- use as many senses as possible in preparing for exams
- start as early as possible set realistic goals and targets
- take advantage of study buddies, study groups, and tutorials
- review previously used exams
- study with positive, knowledgeable, motivated, and supportive individuals
- practice the material in the format in which you are to be tested
- try to simulate the test situation as much as possible
- keep a positive attitude
- end your study time with a quick review and then do something different before you try to go to sleep on the night before the exam
- drink a sufficient amount of water prior to an exam
- stay in the exam room for the full amount of time available
- try to relax by focusing on your breathing

If you combine your best study habits with some of the strategies presented here, you may increase your chances of writing a strong exam and maximizing your potential to do well.

NOTES

Provincial Achievement Test Preparation

A guide to writing the PAT

The *Provincial Achievement Test Preparation* section contains all of the questions from the 2000 and 2001 Provincial Achievement Tests (PATs). The questions presented here are distinct from those in the Unit Review section. It is recommended that students carefully work through these exams as they are reflective of the format and difficulty level of the exam that students are likely to encounter.

THE KEY contains detailed answers that illustrate the problem-solving process for every question in this section.

When writing practice exams, students are encouraged to simulate actual Provincial Achievement Test conditions. This will help students become:

* *aware of the mental and physical stamina required to sit through an entire exam*
* *familiar with the exam format and how the course content is tested*
* *aware of any units or concepts that are troublesome or require additional study*
* *more successful in managing their review effectively*

To simulate the exam conditions students should:

* *use an alarm clock or other timer to monitor the time allowed for the exam*
* *select a quiet writing spot away from all distractions*
* *assemble the appropriate materials that are allowed for writing the exam such as pens, HB pencils, calculator, dictionary*
* *use "test wiseness" skills*
* *complete as much of the exam as possible within the allowable time*

In writing the practice exam students should:

* *read instructions, directions and questions carefully*
* *organize writing time according to the exam emphasis on each section*
* *highlight key words*
* *think about what is being asked*
* *plan their writing; once complete, proof for errors in content, spelling, grammar*
* *watch for bolded words such as most, least, best*
* *in Multiple Choice questions, cross out any choices students know are incorrect*
* *if possible, review all responses upon completion of the exam*

Provincial Achievement Test
Preparation

2000 PROVINCIAL ACHIEVEMENT TEST

INDUSTRIALIZATION AND TECHNOLOGY

1. In automobile manufacturing, the introduction of a moving assembly line was a technological change that increased

   A. employee job satisfaction

   B. costs for the consumer

   C. costs for the worker

   D. worker productivity

2. The use of robotics to make a manufacturing process operate more efficiently is called

   A. innovation

   B. automation

   C. specialization

   D. mechanization

3. In recent years, increasing numbers of people are starting home businesses, which is a form of the

   A. factory system

   B. domestic system

   C. division of labour

   D. specialization of work

4. During the second half of the 20th century, the greatest number of American workers have been employed in

   A. primary industries

   B. secondary industries

   C. tertiary industries

   D. quaternary industries

Use the following information to answer questions 5 and 6.

Debate Over the Effects of Industrialization, 1851

Debater I
The Industrial Revolution has benefited society as a whole. Since 1750, the annual output of our economy has increased seven and a half times. Today, everyone is enjoying things that did not exist a hundred years ago. Railroads have cut travel time and shipping time to one tenth or one twentieth of what they used to be. Telegraphs can send messages across England in seconds. Our tools and our machinery are much improved.

Debater II
There is no doubt that there have been many new inventions in the past hundred years, and that we have increased our total output. But who has actually benefited from all these changes? The rich and the middle classes have become a great deal richer. But the living standards of the vast majority—the working people of this country—have remained the same or have become worse.

—from *The Impact of the Industrial Revolution*

5. The debaters' comments illustrate conflict between

   A. technological advancement and standard of living

   B. improved communication and class structure

   C. worker productivity and job satisfaction

   D. social mobility and quality of life

6. The arguments of Debater II would **most likely** reflect the opinion of

   A. an inventor

   B. an entrepreneur

   C. a factory owner

   D. a factory worker

Use the following headlines to answer question 7.

7. Which of the following questions could be researched using the news stories behind these four headlines?
   - **A.** What part did resources play in industrialization?
   - **B.** What role has labour played in economic growth?
   - **C.** What effects did industrialization have on quality of life?
   - **D.** What roles have innovations played in economic development?

8. Henry Ford made his automobile manufacturing plants more efficient by having workers repeat the same step over and over. This process is known as
   - **A.** automation
   - **B.** specialization
   - **C.** mechanization
   - **D.** industrialization

Use the following information to answer question 9.

One of the most obvious signs of the prosperity of the 1920s was the growth of the automobile industry. Henry Ford dreamed of making an inexpensive car that almost anyone could afford to buy. But if this was to be done, the cost of making cars had to be lowered. Ford decided to apply to car manufacturing a method of mass production that was beginning to be used in some other industries. This method made use of an assembly line, a division of labour, and standardized parts.

—from *Spotlight Canada*

9. Which of the following statements is **best** supported by the information above?
   - **A.** Ford produced automobiles that were reliable.
   - **B.** Ford produced automobiles that changed America.
   - **C.** Ford developed an efficient method to manufacture automobiles.
   - **D.** Ford developed a cheap method to organize labour in the automobile industry.

10. The objective of Stalin's first Five-Year Plan was to
   - **A.** strengthen the military and support the New Economic Policy
   - **B.** encourage private ownership and promote personal gain
   - **C.** reduce imports and achieve national self-sufficiency
   - **D.** develop heavy industry and collectivize agriculture

11. Which of the following pairs of terms is correctly matched?

	Term 1		**Term 2**
A.	New Economic Policy	↔	Public enterprise
B.	Collective farms	↔	Private operations
C.	Five Year Plans	↔	Planned economy
D.	State farms	↔	Private plots

Use the following table to answer questions 12 to 14.

Achievements of the First Five-Year Plan	**1927–28 (actual)**	**1932–33 (plan)**	**1932 (actual)**
National Income (rubles, in 100 millions)	24.4	49.7	45.5
Gross industrial production (rubles, in 100 millions)	18.3	43.2	43.3
• Producers' [capital] goods	6.0	18.1	23.1
• Consumer goods	12.3	25.1	20.2
Gross agricultural production (rubles, in 100 millions)	13.1	25.8	16.6
Electricity (100 m kWs)	5.0	22.0	13.4
Coal (million tonnes)	35.4	75.0	64.3
Oil (million tonnes)	11.7	22.0	21.4
Iron ore (million tonnes)	5.7	19.0	12.1
Pig iron (million tonnes)	3.3	10.0	6.2
Steel (million tonnes)	4.0	10.4	5.9
Super-phosphates (million tonnes)	0.1	3.4	0.6

—adapted from *Stalin's Russia 1924–41*

12. The table indicates that in the first Five-Year Plan

A. gross industrial production more than doubled

B. gross agricultural production doubled

C. coal and oil production doubled

D. pig iron and steel production more than doubled

13. In the years shown, which of the following areas of the economy grew the **least** quickly?

A. National Income

B. Producers' goods

C. Consumer goods

D. Agricultural production

14. The information in the table supports the conclusion that between 1927 and 1932, the Soviet Union

A. concentrated on producing consumer goods

B. remained primarily an agricultural country

C. concentrated on increasing capital goods

D. made rapid industrial progress

Use the following article to answer question 15.

The Space Age
One of the greatest achievements of the Soviet Union was the launching of a satellite to start the Space Age. On October 4, 1957, the Soviet Union sent up an artificial satellite, *Sputnik 1*, to orbit Earth. This historic event surprised the capitalist West and started a "race in space" between the Soviet Union and the United States. Some people used the Soviet Union's achievements in space to argue that communism was better than capitalism.

15. Which of the following inferences is **best** supported by the article?

- **A.** Important innovations can emerge in a centrally planned economy.
- **B.** Significant changes can emerge in a market economy.
- **C.** Industrialization can affect our way of life.
- **D.** Technology can affect our way of life.

16. Which Soviet leader was responsible for the New Economic Policy?

- **A.** Lenin
- **B.** Stalin
- **C.** Khrushchev
- **D.** Gorbachev

17. Which of the following individuals is demonstrating an innovation?

- **A.** A doctor who improves a surgical technique
- **B.** An entrepreneur who starts a restaurant business
- **C.** An accountant who does tax returns for a large business
- **D.** A government inspector who checks the safety of commercial aircraft

Use the following information to answer questions 18 and 19.

Speaker I
Twenty-five years ago, the average person would not have imagined the wonderful types of technology that we use and take for granted every day.

Speaker II
The information highway, the Internet, and other applications of technology create all kinds of opportunities for improving our way of life.

Speaker III
When major technological changes occur without any consideration of their effects, serious societal problems can result.

Speaker IV
People who are unwilling to keep up with technological change will fall by the wayside. They have no one to blame but themselves if they don't take advantage of new technologies.

18. Which two speakers would agree that the consequences of technological change could be negative?

- **A.** Speakers I and II
- **B.** Speakers I and IV
- **C.** Speakers II and III
- **D.** Speakers III and IV

19. With which of the following statements would Speaker IV **most likely** agree?

- **A.** The government should help unemployed workers.
- **B.** The traditional way of performing a task is often the best way.
- **C.** Individuals must be prepared to continue learning throughout their lives.
- **D.** Companies should retrain workers when new technologies are implemented.

Use the following cartoons to answer questions 20 and 21.

Cartoon I

"I'm sorry, Wilson. After 16 years of loyal service, you're being replaced by this microchip."

—from *Canada in a Changing World*

Cartoon II

The company picnic

—from *Pay Cheques & Picket Lines*

20. In Cartoon I, what point is the cartoonist making?

A. Profit is more important than efficiency.

B. Innovation is more important than dedication.

C. Automation is more important than productivity.

D. Specialization is more important than dependability.

21. Both cartoons raise concerns about

A. job security

B. leisure time

C. job satisfaction

D. working conditions

MARKET, CENTRALLY PLANNED, AND MIXED ECONOMIES

22. A person who values individualism would believe that most people

A. can make informed decisions

B. function best in a planned society

C. require guidance to ensure that their goals are achieved

D. should have their choices coordinated to serve the goals of society

23. In a **model** centrally planned economy, the government shows the **most** concern for

A. maintaining freedom

B. the needs of the elite

C. maintaining tradition

D. the needs of the group

Use the following information to answer question 24.

Decisions are made by three groups—consumers, producers, and government. Consumers (buyers) have the right to decide their own goals, where to work, and how and where to spend their money. Producers (sellers) decide what products to produce, how and when to produce them, and whether to go into or get out of a particular business. These decisions are made primarily by buyers and sellers in the marketplace. [Government makes regulations for the common good.]

—from *Our Economy: How It Works*

24. Which type of **model** economy is being described in this information?

A. Mixed economy

B. Market economy

C. Free enterprise economy

D. Centrally planned economy

Use the following information to answer questions 25 to 27.

Speaker I
The state should provide for all citizens. The resources of the state should be shared equally.

Speaker II
The state has no place in the economy. The market should be governed by the laws of supply and demand.

Speaker III
The economy of the state is subject to high and low periods. This is a normal part of the business cycle.

Speaker IV
The state should regulate abuses in the economy. They should set minimum wages, ensure competition, and set safety standards. The market should also play a strong role in the economy.

25. Which two speakers **disagree most** about the role of government in the economy?

A. Speakers I and II

B. Speakers I and IV

C. Speakers II and III

D. Speakers II and IV

26. Which speaker would be **most opposed** to the introduction of wage and price controls?

A. Speaker I

B. Speaker II

C. Speaker III

D. Speaker IV

27. Which speaker would **most likely** be a supporter of a mixed economy?

A. Speaker I

B. Speaker II

C. Speaker III

D. Speaker IV

Use the following statement to answer question 28.

"My goal is to improve employer–employee relations by getting better working conditions. Supporting employees encourages them to be more productive in the workplace."

28. Which of the following individuals would **most likely** make this statement?

A. A worker

B. A consumer

C. A union leader

D. A government official

Use the following cartoon to answer question 29.

"We might get a dog."

—adapted from *Uluschak's Marketplace*

29. This cartoon illustrates the point that in a market economy,

A. scarcity can create consumer demand

B. advertising can create consumer demand

C. consumer demand can create an abundant supply

D. consumer demand can create a reduction in price

30. In Canada, government-owned corporations were formed in order to

A. promote competition in foreign countries

B. encourage foreign investment in the economy

C. supply services not provided by private enterprise

D. prevent large corporations from laying off workers

31. Which of the following developments would most directly concern labour unions?

A. Creation of various forms of artificial life in test tubes

B. Building of satellites capable of launching nuclear weapons

C. Changes in computer technology that force workers out of their jobs

D. Advances in medicine that contribute to an increase in the world's population

32. The economic goals emphasized in a centrally planned economy are

A. efficiency, security, innovation

B. stability, equality, security

C. efficiency, equality, freedom

D. stability, freedom, innovation

Use the following information to answer questions 33 and 34.

Andrew Carnegie was innovative. He did not hesitate to replace equipment made obsolete by new developments, and he hired chemists to find ways of making better steel. At the same time he was not above sharp [unethical] practices. A ruthless competitor, he kept his prices low and in the process drove several steel companies out of business. He joined with other companies to fix prices, then violated the agreements by lowering his own prices. He kept his labor costs low, paying skilled workers ten to twelve dollars a week, barely enough to live on.

—from *Industrialism: The American Experience*

33. When faced with a situation such as the one described above, a government in a **model** market economy would

A. allow companies the freedom to maximize profits

B. provide funds to encourage companies to improve productivity

C. determine the prices companies could charge for their production

D. set wage levels in industry to ensure workers of a good quality of life

34. Which of the following facts supports the conclusion that Andrew Carnegie was innovative?

A. He paid his work force low wages.

B. He found better methods of production.

C. He drove other companies out of business.

D. He joined with other companies to fix prices.

Use the following titles to answer question 35.

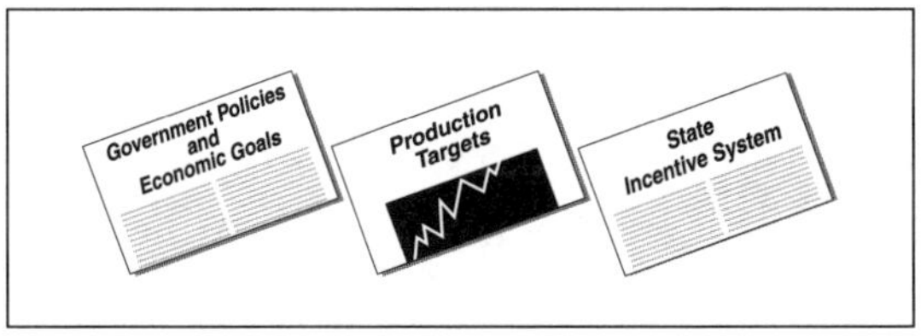

35. Which of the following groups would **most likely** publish this type of information?

A. Labour unions

B. Factory owners

C. Central planners

D. Business entrepreneurs

36. Which of the following model economies is correctly matched with one of its characteristics?

	Model economy		**Character**
A.	Centrally planned economy	↔	Consumer choice
B.	Centrally planned economy	↔	Private initiative
C.	Market economy	↔	Individual freedom
D.	Market economy	↔	Collective good

37. Which of the following characteristics would a centrally planned economy have?

A. High unemployment

B. Controlled prices

C. Business profits

D. Business cycles

38. How would a government in a **model** market economy deal with rising unemployment and poverty during a recession?

A. Purchase key businesses

B. Let the economy recover on its own

C. Set prices and make business accept them

D. Enter into a financial partnership with business

39. Centrally planned economies use a process in which

A. resource industries are controlled by the state

B. decisions about production are made by many producers

C. decisions about production are made by many consumers

D. markets for certain products are controlled by a few producers

Use the following information to answer question 40.

Our government's role is to prevent rapid price changes, limit severe drops in consumer income, and reduce levels of unemployment.

40. A major goal of this government is to promote economic

A. growth

B. equality

C. stability

D. efficiency

41. The basic economic questions faced by every society are

A. how much money should the government issue, who should get the money, and when should they get it

B. what to produce, how to produce, for whom to produce, and how much to produce

C. when to limit the production of harmful products and when to get rid of inefficient workers

D. how the waste of natural resources should be avoided and when the production of capital should be decreased

Use the following cartoon to answer question 42.

—from *The Globe and Mail*

42. Which of the following sayings is **best** supported by the cartoon?

A. The time to stop a revolution is at the beginning, not the end.

B. The more things change, the more they remain the same.

C. The dignity of truth is lost with much protesting.

D. The hungry man is not a free man.

QUALITY OF LIFE

Use the following sources to answer questions 43 and 44.

Source I

Social Indicators in 1992–1993

	Russia	Canada	USA
Population (× 1000)	148 704	27 950	258 328
Births per 1000 people	11.1	14.7	14.5
Deaths per 1000 people	11.9	7.1	8.8
Rate of natural increase	–0.1%	0.7%	0.7%
Infant deaths per 1000 births	17.1	7.0	9.0
Life expectancy			
· For men (in years)	63.3	74.1	72.3
· For women (in years)	74.3	80.9	78.8
Marriages per 1000 people	8.2	7.3	7.7
Divorces per 1000 people	4.1	3.5	3.9
Divorce rate	50.0%	48.0%	51.0%
Doctors per 1000 people	4.8	2.2	2.4
Hospital beds per 1000 people	15.7	6.8	8.4
Crimes per 1000 people	18.5	23.6	31.1
Murders per 10 000 people	9.2	3.5	18.1

Source: *Narodnoe khoziaistvo rossiiskoi federatsii 1992* [National Economy of the Russian Federation 1992].

—from *A New World Emerges*

Source II

Statements

I. Russians have shorter life spans than do Canadians.
II. Canada has better law enforcement than does Russia.
III. Russians receive better health care than do Americans.
IV. Americans commit more crimes than do Canadians

43. The social indicators in Source I are some of the criteria used to assess

A. opportunities for economic growth
B. access to good health care
C. standard of living
D. quality of life

44. Which statements in Source II are **best** supported by information in Source I?

A. I and II
B. I and IV
C. II and III
D. III and IV

Use the following quotes to answer question 45.

"What is the use of a house if you haven't got a tolerable planet to put it on?"

Henry Thoreau, American author

"I realized that if I had to choose, I would rather have birds than airplanes . . ."

Charles Lindberg, the first aviator to make a solo flight across the Atlantic Ocean

45. In both quotes, the speakers raise concerns about

A. technology
B. materialism
C. the environment
D. natural resources

Use the following comment to answer question 46.

I think many office and factory workers would favour more freedom to arrange their work life so they could spend more time with their families. The present five-day workweek could be replaced by allowing workers to choose five six-day weeks in a row followed by a full week off, or people could work a four-day week, but with longer hours each day and work a Saturday once every three or four months.

46. According to the comment, this speaker is concerned about achieving

A. fair wages

B. greater job security

C. increased productivity

D. flexible working arrangements

Use the following cartoon to answer question 47.

—from *The Buffalo News*

47. From the cartoon, it can be inferred that the worker's standard of living will probably

A. decline because of poor labour-management relations

B. improve because he will have other job opportunities

C. decline because he will be unemployed

D. improve because of increased time off

Use the following graphs to answer questions 48 and 49.

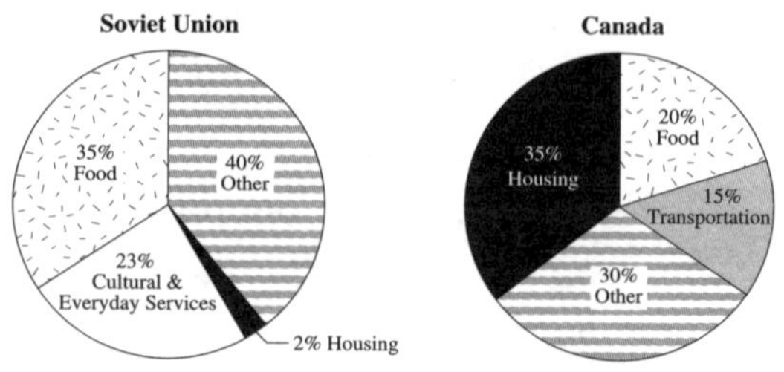

Dividing One's Pay Cheque—1976

—adapted from *The Soviet Union*

48. Which of the following conclusions is supported by the information in these graphs?

A. In 1976, Soviet workers earned approximately the same income as Canadian workers.

B. In 1976, Soviet workers had a higher standard of living because there was no unemployment in the Soviet Union.

C. In 1976, Canadian workers had a higher standard of living because there was a greater variety of products in Canada.

D. In 1976, Canadian workers spent a greater percentage of their income on food and housing combined than did Soviet workers.

49. Which of the following statements **best** explains the large difference in the percentage of wages spent on housing, as shown in the two graphs?

A. In the Soviet Union, the state subsidized housing for its people.

B. In the Soviet Union, there was an oversupply of housing.

C. In Canada, there was a shortage of building materials.

D. In Canada, most cities had a shortage of housing.

50. To someone who believes in a market economy, an important measure of quality of life is the

A. amount of living space that individuals have

B. number of rights that minority groups have

C. degree of free choice that citizens have

D. number of rights that women have

ECONOMIC CHANGE

51. Former Soviet leader Mikhail Gorbachev's policy of perestroika, introduced in 1985, was an attempt to

A. allow factory managers greater input into government decisions

B. restructure the economy to introduce market economy ideas

C. allow individuals increased freedom to criticize the state

D. strengthen the system of central planning of production

Use the following cartoon to answer question 52.

—from *The Edmonton Journal*

52. The point of this cartoon is that reforms in the Soviet Union

A. reduced job opportunities

B. created a large class of entrepreneurs

C. did much to improve the quality of life

D. were slow to solve economic problems

GEOGRAPHY

Use the following maps to answer questions 53 and 54.

Map I

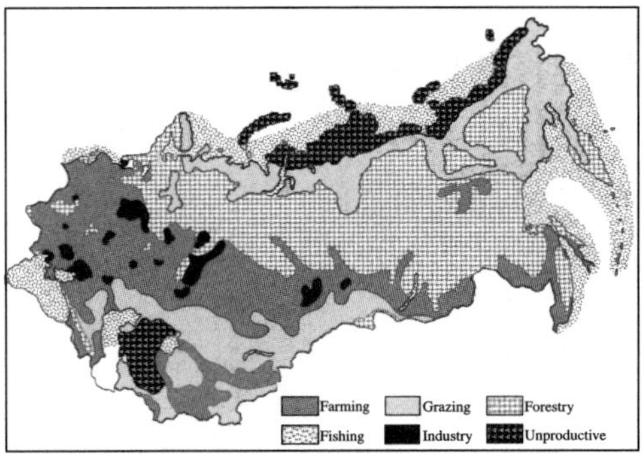

Map II

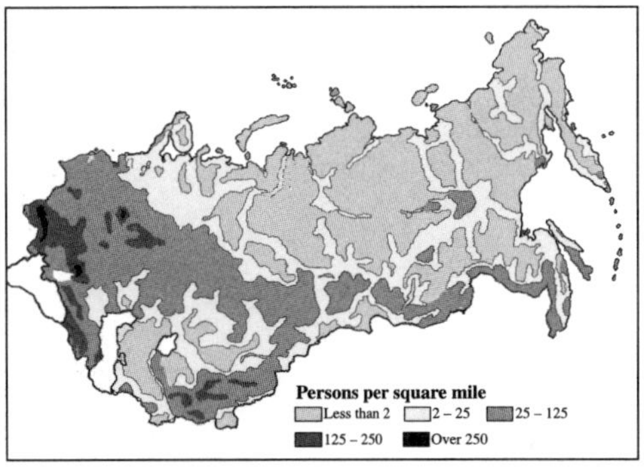

—both maps adapted from *The Soviet Union and Eastern Europe*

53. The maps show that the **majority** of Soviet people were involved in

A. fishing and forestry

B. fishing and industry

C. farming and forestry

D. farming and industry

54. These two maps show

A. land use and population density in the Soviet Union

B. industrial patterns and population size in the Soviet Union

C. agricultural patterns and population size in the Soviet Union

D. landform regions and population density in the Soviet Union

55. The economic development of the Soviet Union was hindered mainly by its

A. lack of natural resources

B. lack of water resources

C. northern location

D. large population

2001 PROVINCIAL ACHIEVEMENT TEST

Note: ***Some questions and solutions are common in both the 2000 and 2001 Provincial Achievement Tests. The common questions and solutions from the 2000 Provincial Achievement Test are not repeated as part of 2001 Provincial Achievement Test for Grade 9 Social Studies. Consequently, the number of questions and solutions appearing for the 2001 Provincial Achievement Test are fewer than the original exam.***

INDUSTRIALIZATION AND TECHNOLOGY

1. The concept of "division of labour" refers to the

A. separating of the production process into small, simple tasks

B. repeating of the same step or series of steps time after time

C. controlling of the size of the workforce

D. training of workers to use many skills

2. Which of the following industries is classified as a secondary industry?

A. Tourism

B. Advertising

C. Manufacturing

D. Transportation

Use the following two illustrations to answer question 3.

Illustration I

Illustration II

—both illustrations from *Witness History Series: The Industrial Revolution*

3. The type of production depicted in Illustration I and the type of production depicted in Illustration II represent the change from

A. an agricultural revolution to an industrial revolution

B. specialized production to mass production

C. unskilled production to skilled production

D. the domestic system to the factory system

4. Which of the following examples **most clearly** involves an innovation?

   A. A doctor who improves a surgical technique

   B. An entrepreneur who starts a restaurant business

   C. An accountant who does tax returns for a large business

   D. A government inspector who checks the safety of commercial aircraft

Use the following comments to answer questions 5 and 6.

Some Views on Genetic Engineering

James Watson
How can we not do it? We used to think our fate was in the stars. Now we know, in large measure, our fate is in our genes. I see an extraordinary potential for human betterment ahead of us. The time to act is now.
(Nobel Prize winner: Co-discoverer of DNA)

Greg Bear
. . . we will have to face the ethical question of just what is a human being and what are the ethical limits of creating new types of human beings.
(Author: Blood Music)

Jeremy Cherfas
Genetic engineering could be used in many ways to make weapons. Bugs more lethal than the ones we already have got would not be difficult to design.
(Author: Man Made Life)

Paul Marango
[Because of genetic engineering, we] can develop . . . drugs that go right to the desired receptors and bypass the others. That means they won't have a lot of side effects.
(Biochemist)

—from *Canada: Towards the 21st Century*

5. Which two speakers raise concerns about the dangers of genetic engineering?

   A. James Watson and Greg Bear

   B. James Watson and Paul Marango

   C. Greg Bear and Jeremy Cherfas

   D. Jeremy Cherfas and Paul Marango

6. Which of the following issues do all four comments address?

   A. Should the development of technology be a means of promoting economic growth?

   B. Should the development of technology be a means of creating employment?

   C. Should technology be used to make humans more efficient?

   D. Should technology be used to alter nature?

Use the following graphs to answer question 7.

Soviet Production in Key Industries, 1915– 63

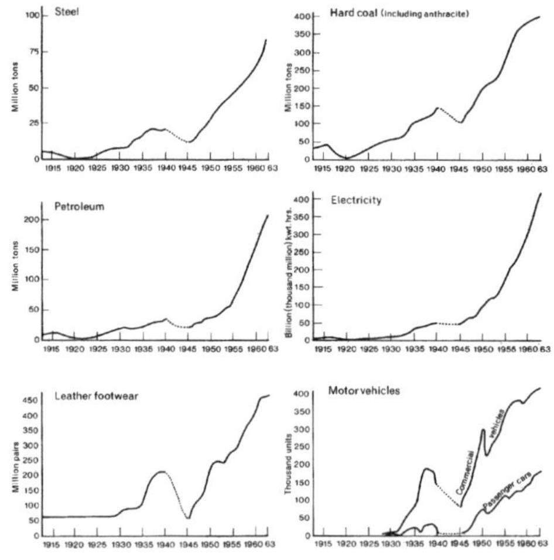

—from *World Powers in the Twentieth Century*

7. A conclusion that can be made from the information in the graphs is that between 1915 and 1963, industrial production in the Soviet Union
   - **A.** mainly stressed the development of consumer goods
   - **B.** increased in a number of sectors of the economy
   - **C.** rapidly improved the Soviet standard of living
   - **D.** increased as a result of consumer demand

Use the following statement to answer question 8.

It is sometimes necessary to take one step backward so that we can take two steps forward.

8. This idea was used by Lenin to support the introduction of
   - **A.** perestroika
   - **B.** centralization
   - **C.** the Five-Year Plans
   - **D.** the New Economic Policy

Use the following speech to answer question 9.

From a Speech by Stalin in February 1931
It is sometimes asked whether it is not possible to slow down the tempo somewhat,
to put a check on the movement. No, comrades, it is not possible! The tempo must not be reduced! . . . To slacken the tempo would mean falling behind. And those who fall behind get beaten. No, we refuse to be beaten . . .
We are 50 or 100 years behind the advanced countries. We must make good this distance in ten years. Either we do it, or we shall be crushed.

—from *Russia and the USSR: 1905–56*

9. Which of the following terms identifies the economic goal Stalin was promoting?
   - **A.** Industrialization
   - **B.** Centralization
   - **C.** Collectivism
   - **D.** Materialism

10. In the Soviet Union, the collectivization of agriculture was introduced by
    - **A.** Trotsky
    - **B.** Stalin
    - **C.** Lenin
    - **D.** Marx

MARKET, CENTRALLY PLANNED, AND MIXED ECONOMIES

11. Which of the following economic systems experiences the lowest unemployment rates?
    - **A.** Centrally planned economy
    - **B.** Capitalist economy
    - **C.** Market economy
    - **D.** Mixed economy

Use the following statement to answer question 12.

Many [people] have forgotten that we set up regulatory agencies in the first place in order to protect the public interest. Industries considered vital to the public—such as transportation, food, finance, communications, and nuclear power—were regulated in order to provide the public a steady flow of safe products in a stable environment.

—from *Economics in America: Opposing Viewpoints*

12. The situation described in the statement above **most likely** occurred in a

A. mixed economy

B. traditional economy

C. model market economy

D. model centrally planned economy

Use the following statements to answer questions 13 and 14.

Statement I	Individuals provide their own resources (their capital, their labour, their land) to businesses in exchange for money.
Statement II	Individuals own the resources. Private producers combine the resources to produce goods and services that are then sold to consumers.
Statement III	Governments regulate some aspects of the economy and supply particular services to individuals and businesses. Governments are also consumers because they buy certain goods and services from businesses.
Statement IV	Governments own all of the factors of production and means of distribution of goods and services.

13. The statement **most clearly** related to a centrally planned economy is

A. Statement I

B. Statement II

C. Statement III

D. Statement IV

14. The statement **most clearly** related to a mixed economy is

A. Statement I

B. Statement II

C. Statement III

D. Statement IV

Use the following cartoon to answer question 15.

—from *Looking Forward*

15. The cartoonist is suggesting that

A. every economic system has disadvantages

B. market economies are better than communism

C. consumers have more choice in a market system

D. capitalism is superior to centrally planned economies

16. A term that can be used to describe the economic condition that results when wants are greater than the resources available to satisfy them is

A. greed

B. scarcity

C. limited needs

D. unlimited wants

17. In a **model** market economy, the government

A. prevents monopolies from forming

B. avoids involvement in the economy

C. provides a social safety net for its citizens

D. intervenes in the economy during times of depression

Use the following information to answer question 18.

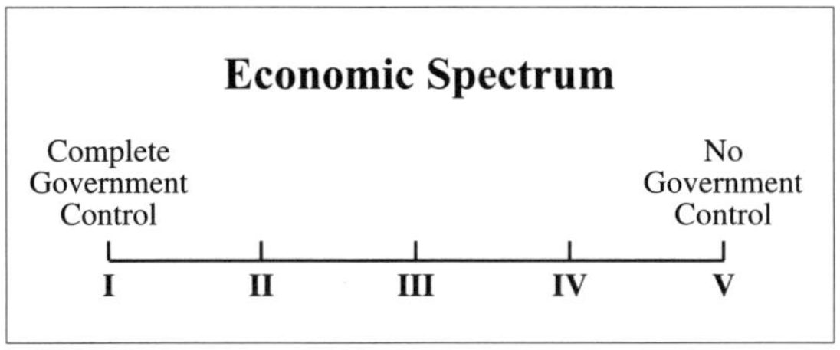

18. In the economic system that is represented by Position IV on the spectrum above, it is **most likely** that

A. consumer choices are planned by the state

B. wages are determined by the market

C. the state is the only employer

D. competition is prohibited

19. Government intervention in union negotiations would **most likely** occur in a

A. model centrally planned economy

B. model market economy

C. traditional economy

D. mixed economy

Use the following information to answer question 20.

> The governments draw up plans, decide how much of everything is to be produced, and send out directives to the producers. Nice and neat, except when you happen to want a new pair of shoes and the factories are only producing boots.

—from *Sunshine Sketches of a Little Economics*

20. What type of economic system is referred to in this information?

A. Centrally planned economy

B. Traditional economy

C. Market economy

D. Mixed economy

21. What type of economic system takes measures to achieve a balance between economic freedom and stability?

A. Centrally planned economy

B. Traditional economy

C. Market economy

D. Mixed economy

Use the following information to answer question 22.

Some Reasons for Economic Problems in the Soviet Union

- Central decision-making meant little incentive for local factories to make improvements.
- Agriculture, factories and raw materials were located thousands of kilometres apart, leading to wasteful transportation of materials and goods between them.
- Scarce resources were channeled into military production.
- As a result of industrial and agricultural problems, the price of food rose much faster than wages.

—adapted from *The Breakup of the Soviet Union*

22. The **best** conclusion that can be drawn from the above information is that in the Soviet Union,

A. consumers had little freedom of choice

B. the centrally planned economy was inefficient

C. there was little motivation for efficient management

D. the centrally planned economy stifled individual effort

QUALITY OF LIFE

Use the following cartoons to answer question 23.

Cartoon I

Cartoon II

—both cartoons from *The Victoria Times-Colonist*

23. The two cartoons illustrate the conflict between

A. productivity and progress

B. materialism and quality of life

C. entrepreneurship and quality of life

D. economic growth and environmentalism

Use the following comments to answer questions 24 and 25.

Speaker I
My quality of life is tied to a good lifestyle. Without a steady income, I would feel worthless. The more money I make, the better my quality of life will be.

Speaker II
My quality of life is based on how I feel about myself. For me, this means a sound mind and body. If I were absolutely poor, I would still have a high quality of life because I am happy with who I am.

Speaker III
My quality of life is tied to many things: my job, my family, my religion. The best quality of life comes when people have a balanced life.

Speaker IV
My quality of life is based on being healthy and knowing that others respect me. Only those who are really healthy can have a good quality of life.

24. Which of the following pairs of speakers would **most closely** agree with each other's comments on what makes up a good quality of life?

A. Speakers I and II

B. Speakers I and III

C. Speakers II and IV

D. Speakers III and IV

25. Which speaker's quality of life would **most likely** decline as a result of the government increasing taxes?

A. Speaker I

B. Speaker II

C. Speaker III

D. Speaker IV

26. The **greatest difference** in standard of living between individuals in a market economy and those in a centrally planned economy is in the area of

A. educational opportunities

B. religious freedom

C. material wealth

D. health care

ECONOMIC CHANGE

27. From 1985 to 1991, Mikhail Gorbachev's attempts at economic reform in the Soviet Union were focused on

A. creating a free market economy

B. building a public enterprise economy

C. preserving a centrally planned economy

D. introducing a modified market economy

Use the following cartoon to answer question 29.

—from *The Washington Times*

28. This cartoon about the Soviet Union illustrates the

A. confusion that people had about how the economic system worked

B. inefficiency of the economic system in meeting basic needs

C. need for people to be organized to produce goods

D. problems caused by urban overpopulation

ANSWERS AND SOLUTIONS
2000 PROVINCIAL ACHIEVEMENT TEST

1.	D	11.	C	21.	A	31.	C	41.	B	51.	B
2.	B	12.	A	22.	A	32.	B	42.	B	52.	D
3.	B	13.	D	23.	D	33.	A	43.	D	53.	D
4.	C	14.	D	24.	A	34.	B	44.	B	54.	A
5.	A	15.	A	25.	A	35.	C	45.	C	55.	C
6.	D	16.	A	26.	B	36.	C	46.	D		
7.	D	17.	A	27.	D	37.	B	47.	C		
8.	B	18.	D	28.	C	38.	B	48.	D		
9.	C	19.	C	29.	B	39.	A	49.	A		
10.	D	20.	B	30.	C	40.	C	50.	C		

1. D

A. The tasks each worker was assigned were simple and repetitive all day long.

B. The cost of automobiles was reduced due to the introduction of the assembly line.

C. Worker costs went down because the skills each worker needed in the industry became less important due to specialization of labour.

D. The assembly line sped up the process and the number of automobiles greatly increased, thus making each worker more productive.

2. B

A. Innovation is the creation of new technology from combining existing technologies together.

B. The use of robots or computers to do the work that humans used to do is called automation.

C. Specilization is when workers are given a narrow set of tasks and skills to make them more efficient.

D. Mechanization is the use of machines to do work that used to be done by hand.

3. B

A. The factory system focuses the means of production in a central place and labour goes to work at this site.

B. The main element of the domestic system is that the worker labours in their home and does not travel to a workplace to do their job.

C. The division of labour is the break down of a complex task into separate and more simple tasks. Each worker is responsible for only one part of the whole process.

D. Specialization of work is when workers are given a narrow set of tasks and skills to make them more efficient.

4. C

A. The number of workers in primary industries has been reduced during the second half of the 20th Century.

B. The number of workers in secondary industries has been reduced during the second half of the 20th Century.

C. Most people worked in tertiary industries of the economy in the second half of the 20th Century.

D. Quaternary industries are a new and growing area of the economy but the number of people involved in them are quite small.

5. A

A. Both sources are discussing the development of technology and the living standard of people in society.

B. One source mentions communication and the other mentions class structure.

C. No mention of these topics in the sources.

D. No mention of social mobility in either source.

6. D

A. See D.

B. See D.

C. See D.

D. The most likely opinion would be of a factory worker because the benefits described favoured the inventor, entrepreneur, and factory owner.

7. D

A. Only two of the headlines talk about inventions and resources directly. The other two relate to secondary or tertiary industries not primary.

B. There is no mention of labour in any of the headlines.

C. There is no mention of the positive or negative effects of industrialization the on quality of life.

D. Every one of these headlines is an innovation that leads to economic development.

8. B

A. Automation is the use of robots to do work formerly done by people.

B. Specialization is the reduction of a task into a very specific action or skill. This allows a worker to do one specific task over and over again.

C. Mechanization is the use of machines to do work formerly done by hand.

D. Industrialization is a concept that involves many different factors such as urbanization, the factory system, and mechanization not just the repetition of the same step over and over again.

9. C

A. There is no mention of reliability in the reading.

B. There is no mention of a change in America.

C. Assembly line, division of labour, and standardized parts are all way to increase the efficiency of production.

D. The paragraph describes a manufacturing process that includes standardized parts. Standardized parts have nothing to do with the organization of labour which makes C a better answer.

10. D

A. Lenin created the New Economic Policy and Stalin did nothing to support it.

B. Stalin never supported any form of private ownership and didn't promote personal gain.

C. These are not goals of the First Five-Year Plan.

D. Stalin moved away from any private ownership of land (collectivization of agriculture) and set targets for industrial development.

11. C

A. The New Economic Policy allowed for some private enterprise to exist.

B. Collective farms are owned by the state and can't be privately owned.

C. Five-Year Plans were economic plans started by Stalin. The government set production targets and expected its citizens to meet them.

D. State farms are owned by the government not private individuals.

12. A

A. From the table, actual gross industrial production doubled from 18.3 to 43.3.

B. Gross agricultural production did not double.

C. Based on actual figures coal and oil did not double.

D. Based on actual figures pig iron and steel did not double.

Note: It is important to read the chart carefully and focus on actual figures and not get confused by plan numbers.

13. D

A. National income almost doubled. This is faster growth than D.

B. Producers' goods more than doubled. This is faster growth than D.

C. Consumer goods rose by around 8. This is faster growth than D.

D. Agricultural production only increased by 3.5. This is the smallest increase of the four choices.

14. D

A. The table does not show a significant increase in consumer goods.

B. The large gains in industrial production contradict this choice.

C. The table shows concentration on a wide variety of products.

D. When looking at all the information from the table, many areas of the economy that are needed to create industrial progress, such as electricity, oil, pig iron, superphosphate, etc., all tell of increases in production.

15. A

A. The launching of Sputnik was an innovation and it happened in the centrally planned economy of the USSR.

B. There is no mention of a market economy or changes in a market economy.

C. The article does not deal with the issue of industrialization or its effects.

D. The article deals with a Soviet accomplishment not its affect on our lives.

16. A

A. Lenin was forced to implement the New Economic Policy when War Communism failed.

B. Stalin moved away from the New Economic Policy.

C. Krushchev had nothing to do with the New Economic Policy.

D. Gorbachev had nothing to do with the New Economic Policy.

17. A

A. Innovation is a change in a product or task for the better. Improving a surgical technique is making something better.

B. This is an example of somebody doing a job. There is no mention of change.

C. This is an example of somebody doing a job. There is no mention of change.

D. This is an example of somebody doing a job. There is no mention of change.

18. D

A. Speakers I and II use words like 'wonderful' and 'amazing' in their statements. These are not negative words.

B. Speaker I has a positive tone and Speaker IV has a negative tone.

C. Speaker II has a positive tone and Speaker III has a negative tone.

D. Both speakers III and IV use words like "problems" and "blame". These two speakers both have negative tones.

19. C

A. There is no mention about how people were to 'keep up' or who these people are, 'unemployed' or not.

B. The message seems to say that change is going to happen, no mention of traditional ways, good or bad.

C. 'Individuals' relates to 'people' in the Speaker's comments, and the idea 'to continue learning' relates to 'keeping up' from the text.

D. This only deals with 'companies' and 'workers' while Speaker IV talks in a very general way with the term 'people'.

20. B

A. There is no mention in the cartoon of profit or efficiency.

B. The microchip is a change (Innovation) which replaces the dedicated (loyal) employee.

C. There is no mention of the productivity level of the employee, and why would a company automate if it didn't increase productivity?

D. There is no evidence to show what tasks the worker did or how specialized the tasks are.

21. A

A. In both cartoons, workers are or have been replaced with new technology. This represents a serious lack of job security.

B. There is no leisure time represented in the first cartoon.

C. Job satisfaction is not shown positively or negatively in either cartoon.

D. Neither cartoon comments on working conditions.

22. A

A. Individualism is the belief in the rights and abilities of the individual.

B. A planned society supports collectivism, which is the opposite of individualism.

C. A person who values individualism would believe that individuals can reach their goals on their own.

D. The goals of society concern the whole group not the individual.

23. D

A. Freedom is associated with the goals of the model market economy.

B. In a model centrally planned economy there is no elite group or class.

C. Centrally planned economies represent a shift from traditions.

D. The main concern of the model centrally planned economy is to take care of the needs of the group.

24. A

A. By involving the government, consumers, and producers, this becomes a mixed economy.

B. A model market economy would not include government.

C. A model free enterprise system would not include government.

D. A model centrally planned economy would not include consumers and producers.

25. A

A. Speaker I is supporting a centrally planned economy while Speaker II is more in line with a market economy.

B. Speaker I is supporting a centrally planned economy while Speaker IV discusses a mixed economy. These are not opposites as with A.

C. Both of these speakers are advocating for a market economy.

D. Speaker II is supporting a market economy while Speaker IV is supporting a mixed economy. These are not opposites.

26. B

A. Speaker I wants the state to be involved in the economy.

B. Speaker II clearly states that the 'state has no place in the economy'.

C. Speaker III doesn't clearly state that the government absolutely should not introduce wage and price control.

D. Speaker IV advocates for a minimum wage, which is a wage control.

27. D

A. Speaker I wants to give a lot of control to the government and makes no reference to aspects of the market system.

B. Speaker II is clear that no level of state involvement is good.

C. There is no position given for the state, so only the market is applied to the economy.

D. Key roles for the market and government in the economy are clearly given by Speaker IV.

28. C

A. A worker's responsibility is to do a job and make money, not to improve employee-employer relations.

B. A consumer's goal is to get good quality products at the best price, not to improve employee-employer relations.

C. A union leader's purpose is to protect working conditions and negotiate with employers.

D. A Government Official is less likely to get involved in individual businesses relationships with their workers unless they have to.

29. B

A. In the cartoon there seems to be a lot of dog food so it would not create consumer demand in this way.

B. The sign and the low price on it point to the odd idea that the consumer is buying dog food but doesn't own a dog; this tries to show the power of advertising.

C. This is unlikely. If anything, high consumer demand would lead to a decrease in supply.

D. Higher demand would generally create an increase in price not a decrease.

30. C

A. Canada does not involve itself in the promotion of competition in foreign countries.

B. Government-owned corporations are not formed to encourage foreign investment in the economy.

C. Canada has a large land mass and small, spread out population. Because it was not profitable for private enterprise to provide certain necessary services, the Government formed crown corporations to do so.

D. The government might try and encourage a corporation to keep employees but it wouldn't form a new corporation to keep those people employed.

31. C

A. Labour unions would not involve themselves in research into creating artificial life forms.

B. Labour unions would not concern themselves with political issues.

C. Labour unions are primarily concerned with the worker's ability to stay employed. They would fight against technology that eliminated jobs.

D. Increased population is not a labour issue. Increased employment resulting from increased population would be of interest to a labour union.

32. B

A. Efficiency is often lacking in centrally planned economies.

B. Stability, equality and security are all goals of centrally planned economies.

C. Goals of efficiency, equality and freedom are associated with market economies.

D. Freedom is not a goal of centrally planned economies.

33. A

A. A model market economy values freedom. It also has no government involvement.

B. Government funding is not part of a model market economy.

C. Determining prices is government intervention and is discouraged in a model market economy.

D. Setting wages is another example of government intervention.

34. B

A. Paying low wages is not a change for the better.

B. Better methods of production is an example of an innovation because it is a change intended to improve production.

C. Putting companies out of business is not a change for the better.

D. Price fixing is not a positive change.

35. C

A. Labour unions wouldn't be involved in this because they don't set government policies or production targets.

B. The State refers to the government. Factory owners and business people wouldn't be creating incentive systems for the government.

C. The job of central planners is to set targets, determine economic goals, and to create state incentives.

D. See B.

36. C

A. A wide range of consumer choice is not a characteristic of a centrally planned economy because of its emphasis on capital goods.

B. A planned economy does not lend itself too much for private enterprise.

C. Individual freedom is a basic element of the market system for both consumers and business people.

D. A market system directs itself towards individual good more so than collective good.

37. B

A. The plan in a centrally planned economy is directed toward full employment for the people, not high unemployment.

B. All aspects of the economy are planned, including the price of goods.

C. Profits are not one of the end goals of a centrally planned economy.

D. Due to the planning of a central economy there should not be a business cycle like the one you would find in a market economy.

38. B

A. In a model market economy the government doesn't own businesses.

B. In a model market economy there is no place for government intervention.

C. Governments in a model market economy don't set prices or force businesses to accept them.

D. Governments in a model market economy don't enter into partnerships with businesses.

39. A

A. State ownership and control are important aspects of centrally planned economies.

B. Producers make decisions in market economies.

C. Consumers make decisions in market economies.

D. Markets are controlled by the government in centrally planned economies.

40. C

A. Price increases could be seen as a sign of growth.

B. Equality is not explicitly clear in the example.

C. Essentially the government is promoting stability by preventing sudden drastic change in the market.

D. Efficiency is not explicitly present in the example.

41. B

A. See B.

B. The answer for B has all of the basic economic questions that any economy has to answer. What to produce? How to Produce? For whom to Produce? How much to Produce? The other answers do not have any of the basic questions in them.

C. See B.

D. See B.

42. B

A. The cartoon has no beginning or end.

B. The Russian people are marching around in a big circle suggesting that nothing has changed since the Russian Revolution.

C. There is no evidence of lost truth or protesting.

D. The round shapes of the figures and the bags they are carrying don't seem to indicate hungry people.

43. D

A. None of the indicators specifically lead to economic growth.

B. Not all of the indicators deal with health care. Divorce, crime, and marriages are not health care related.

C. Standard of living is part of Quality of Life that deals more with the quality of consumer products and the ability to purchase them.

D. Quality of Life is assessed by the criteria indicated in the sources.

44. B

A. Russians do have shorter life spans but Canada has more crime.

B. Russians do have shorter life spans than Canadians and America has more crime than Canada.

C. Canada does not necessarily have better law enforcement and Russians do not receive better health care.

D. Russian's have shorter life expectancy, a higher death rate, and more infant deaths than do Americans.

45. C

A. In Thoreau's quotation there is no real reference to technology.

B. There isn't enough information about having or owning a lot of homes, or many airplanes, etc… to have the quotation raise issues about materialism.

C. References common to both speakers such as 'tolerable planet' and 'rather have birds than airplanes' relate to the environment.

D. No reference toward natural resources can be directly made from the information.

46. D

A. There is no discussion from the Speaker concerning wages.

B. There is no discussion from the Speaker concerning greater job security.

C. There is no discussion from the Speaker concerning increased productivity.

D. The Speaker is discussing the work schedule, offering several different choices workers could choose.

47. C

A. Labour-management relations are more than 'poor' in the cartoon. In the cartoon the relationship has ended.

B. From the cartoon there is no indication of any other job opportunities.

C. The worker will not be paid a wage. Notice the little figures of the bottom right-hand side, the 'a vacation from pay' and the worker saying 'I'm fired right?' Both support him being unemployed.

D. From the cartoon you can not determine that his standard of living will improve because of increased time off.

48. D

A. The graph only deals with how the wages were spent not with how much a person was paid.

B. Neither graph deals with the amount of employment in either country.

C. The graphs do not indicate the number of products available in each country.

D. Canadian spending on food and housing equals 55% while the Soviets spent 37%.

49. A

A. The Soviet government built and subsidized all of the housing and could keep the costs down.

B. Many people had to share housing in the Soviet Union.

C. Canada has many natural resources, which are used for building materials.

D. Even if there was a shortage of housing in 1976, which there wasn't, it wouldn't explain a difference of 33%.

50. C

A. The measure of living space is only one, very small measurement when you are measuring quality of life.

B. Somebody who supported a market economy would view this as government intervention and is more political than economic.

C. 'Free Choice' in the market is very important to a person who supports a free market economy.

D. This would be viewed as government intervention and is more political than economic.

51. B

A. Under the centrally planned Soviet system, the factory managers already had some input with the government but perestroika was introduced to change who made the decisions in the economy.

B. Perestroika is the restructuring of the economy to improve the Soviet economy by introducing some market system ideas in the economy.

C. This is not an economic freedom introduced by Gorbachev. This is glasnost, a political reform introduced by Gorbachev.

D. The system of perestroika was to change the central planning system by taking some economic planning away from the government and giving to others in Soviet society.

52. D

A. From the cartoon source there is no indication of reduced job opportunities.

B. From the cartoon source there is no indication of a created class of entrepreneurs.

C. With the 'where's the beef' quotation, the cartoon doesn't give the impression of any improvement in the quality of life.

D. The cartoon has the leader of the Soviet Union, Mikhail Gorbachev, serving behind a counter of a McDonald's Restaurant. The message from the cartoon is even if the Soviet economy has changed toward a more western market economy style, the caption 'where's the beef' shows that the reforms and changes are not solving economic problems such as consumer goods.

53. D

A. When you compare the two maps you find that not many people are located where fishing is the main economic activity.

B. See A.

C. When you compare the two maps you find that not many people are located where forestry is the main economic activity.

D. From the two map sources when you compare where most of the people are located and what main economic activities are in those regions you see they are farming and industry.

54. A

A. The first map deals with land uses and the second map has population density. In the first map there is mention of both agricultural and industrial uses. The second map expresses population per square mile. This is an expression of population density.

B. The first map has agricultural and industrial land use not just agriculture.

C. The first map has industrial and agricultural uses not just industrial.

D. There is no mention of landforms in either map.

55. C

A. The Soviet Union had ample natural resources due to its large size.

B. The Soviet Union had many rivers and lakes.

C. The northern location made it difficult to collect and transport many of its ample resources.

D. A large population would not harm the development of the Soviet Union. More likely, it would provide a large workforce for development.

ANSWERS AND SOLUTIONS
2001 PROVINCIAL ACHIEVEMENT TEST

Note: ***Some questions and solutions are common in both the 2000 and 2001 Provincial Achievement Tests. The common questions and solutions from the 2000 Provincial Achievement Test are not repeated as part of 2001 Provincial Achievement Test for Grade 9 Social Studies. Consequently, the number of questions and solutions appearing for the 2001 Provincial Achievement Test are fewer than the original exam.***

1.	**A**	**6.**	**D**	**11.**	**A**	**16.**	**B**	**21.**	**D**	**26.**	**C**
2.	**C**	**7.**	**B**	**12.**	**A**	**17.**	**B**	**22.**	**B**	**27.**	**D**
3.	**D**	**8.**	**D**	**13.**	**D**	**18.**	**B**	**23.**	**D**	**28**	**B**
4.	**A**	**9.**	**A**	**14.**	**C**	**19.**	**D**	**24.**	**C**		
5.	**C**	**10**	**B**	**15.**	**A**	**20.**	**A**	**25.**	**A**		

1. A

A. This process means that fewer skills are needed and more products can be produced. Each worker is only responsible for a portion of the product, not the whole item.

B. This choice seems close but is incorrect because it is not specific enough. All crafts people, workers, and technicians repeat the same steps or series of steps, not just those that are dealing with division of labour.

C. Controlling the size of the workforce has nothing to do with the question.

D. This concept usually means a reduction of the number of skills a worker uses, not an increase in skills.

2. C

A. Tourism exists to provide services to people who are visiting a new place. Providing a service is a tertiary industry.

B. Advertising provides clients with commercials, ads, or brands. This is an example of providing a service, which makes this a tertiary industry.

C. Turning raw materials into finished products is called Secondary industry or Manufacturing.

D. The movement of people, products, and ideas is a service and is therefore a tertiary industry.

3. D

A. The picture does not show the creation of agriculture or even a change in agricultural methods.

B. Specialization would be part of mass production and wouldn't be a change.

C. The person in the first picture is using skill so cannot be considered unskilled.

D. The domestic system, work done at home or cottage, is shown in the first picture and the second picture shows a factory full of machines.

4. A

A. Innovation is a change in a product or task for the better. Improving a surgical technique is making something better.

B. This is an example of somebody doing a job. There is no mention of change.

C. This is an example of somebody doing a job. There is no mention of change.

D. This is an example of somebody doing a job. There is no mention of change.

5. C

A. James Watson talks of the "extraordinary potential" and is very positive.

B. Paul Marango talks of the positive effects on drugs and the reduction of side effects.

C. These two speakers raise issues about ethical limits and the possibility of lethal bugs, and both are concerned about negative effects.

D. See B.

6. D

A. There is no direct mention of economic growth in the comments.

B. There is no mention of job creation.

C. Greg Bear comments on the idea of being human but doesn't mention efficiency. Jeremy Cherfas makes no mention of humans at all.

D. This is the answer because all of the speakers comment on either positive or negative effects of altering nature.

7. B

A. Consumer goods are only represented in two of the six graphs.

B. All of these graphs are increasing and several areas of the economy are represented.

C. There is no mention of standard of living in the graphs. It is unlikely that an increase in hard coal or steel would have rapidly improved the Soviet standard of living.

D. Consumer demand was not considered by the Soviet government, and is not represented by the graphs.

8. D

A. Perestroika was a policy or restructuring brought in by Gorbachev.

B. Centralization was not one of Lenin's policies.

C. The Five-Year Plans were Stalin's policy.

D. The New Economic Policy was Lenin's Policy and it allowed for some private enterprise.

9. A

A. Stalin's goal was to Industrialize the USSR as quickly as possible.

B. Centralization was not something that the Soviets needed to catch up with in regards to more advanced countries.

C. Collectivization was not practiced in more advanced countries.

D. The USSR did not want to promote or increase materialism.

10. B

A. Trotsky was not associated with the idea of collectivization.

B. One of Stalin's first policies was the collectivization of agriculture.

C. Lenin had to move away from collectivization when War Communism failed.

D. Karl Marx was a philosopher and wasn't involved in the policies of the Soviet Union.

11. A

A. Centrally planned societies can ensure through the government that all citizens have employment.

B. Capitalist economies value freedom and risk. This ensures a certain level of unemployment.

C. A Market economy is basically the same as a capitalist economy. It allows for the freedom to not work and lacks government intervention to create jobs when there are none.

D. Mixed economies are a mixture of both major economic systems. Therefore there might be some government intervention but not enough to eliminate unemployment altogether.

12. A

A. A Mixed Economy has some market tendencies and some planned tendencies. The statement allows for private ownership but with regulatory agencies. This is a combination of both economic systems.

B. A Traditional Economy is based on the traditions of the past. It would deal setting up new agencies or even modern economic problems.

C. A model is an ideal representation of something. A Model Market Economy would have no government regulation.

D. A Model Centrally Planned Economy would not have any privately owned businesses. They would be owned and controlled by the government in the beginning.

13. D

A. Individuals owning their own resources and deciding where to distribute them is not associated with central planning.

B. Producers and consumers meeting in the market to buy and sell goods is not associated with central planning.

C. Governments in central planning would not have to buy from businesses.

D. Governments in centrally planned economies own all of the production and distribution of goods and services.

14. C

A. Statement I has individuals making choices in the market without any government involvement.

B. Statement II has producers and consumers meeting in the market without any government involvement.

C. Statement III has a mixture of government regulation and private ownership.

D. Statement IV has government ownership without choice or private ownership.

15. A

A. Communism has just crumbled because it was flawed. Capitalism has arrived. People are lining up at soup kitchens. Both systems have flaws so the cartoonist is suggesting that every system has disadvantages.

B. If the cartoonist is suggesting that market economies are better than communism the cartoon wouldn't show people lining up at a soup kitchen. They would be eating in a fine restaurant.

C. The people lining up at the soup kitchen are not being given any choices.

D. See B.

16. B

A. Greed doesn't deal with the lack of resources only the desire to have them.

B. Scarcity is when you have more wants than resources. Unlimited wants + limited resources = Scarcity.

C. Limited needs would lead to a decrease in scarcity.

D. Unlimited wants is only half of the problem.

17. B

A. In a model market economy the government would not involve itself in the prevention of monopoly formation.

B. The model market economy has no government intervention in the market.

C. A social safety net would require government involvement.

D. The model market economy has no government intervention in the market.

18. B

A. State planning is an example of government control and would be closer to Position I.

B. There is no mention of any kind of government control. Wages are being determined by market forces.

C. If the state is the only employer that gives the government a lot of power and control.

D. The prohibition of competition is an example of government control.

19. D

A. In a model centrally planned economy the government would be the employer and wouldn't allow unions.

B. In a model market economy the government would have no involvement in the economy.

C. Traditional economies don't usually have unions or government intervention into unions.

D. The presence of government intervention suggests that the government doesn't automatically own everything, but is not against involving itself in the economy. This indicates that this is most likely a mixed economy.

20. A

- **A. Governments planning what and how to make products is part of central planning of production.**
- B. Decisions in traditional economies are made based on old traditions not the desires of the government.
- C. Decisions are made by producers and consumers in the market economy.
- D. There is no evidence of a combination of economic systems.

21. D

- A. Centrally planned economies do not have economic freedom.
- B. Traditional economies exist because that is the way they have always existed.
- C. Market economies do not encourage economic stability.
- **D. Mixed economies have some level of economic freedom and stability.**

22. B

- A. Freedom of choice is not mentioned in any of the statements.
- **B. Improvements could make farms efficient. Long distances between raw materials and manufacturing sites were inefficient. An inability of wages to react to price increases also indicates inefficiency.**
- C. Motivation is only mentioned as an incentive in one of the statements.
- D. There is no mention of stifling individual effort in any of the statements.

23. D

- A. There is no evidence of productivity in either cartoon.
- B. There is no evidence of the accumulation of consumer goods.
- C. There is no evidence of entrepreneurship in the second cartoon.
- **D. Both cartoons deal clearly with environmentalism and the consequences of economic growth on the environment, like developing the wilderness for tourism.**

24. C

- A. Speaker I needs money to be happy and Speaker II doesn't. They disagree.
- B. Speaker I needs money. Speaker III needs a balanced life and doesn't mention money. They disagree.
- **C. Speaker II and IV both talk about their own individual selves. They are more likely to agree.**
- D. Speaker III would be willing to sacrifice a little of her/his health to improve the family or job; Speaker IV would not. They disagree.

25. A

- **A. Speaker I values money above all else. Taxes would reduce the amount of money that could define the worth of the speaker.**
- B. Speaker II doesn't mention money.
- C. Speaker III doesn't mention money.
- D. Speaker IV doesn't mention money.

26. C

A. Education is typically associated with quality of life, and is not necessarily lower in either economic system.

B. Religious freedom is typically associated with quality of life, and is not an economic issue.

C. Material wealth is a determiner of standard of living. Material wealth is economic in nature and very different between market and centrally planned economies.

D. Health care is typically associated with quality of life, and is not necessarily different between economic systems.

27. D

A. Gorbachev wanted to change the Soviet Union slowly, while still preserving aspects of the Soviet system. He didn't want to go into a free market system.

B. A public enterprise system is essentially the same as answer A.

C. Gorbachev knew that the centrally planned economy needed changing. He didn't want to preserve it. He wanted to change it carefully.

D. Gorbachev wanted a modified market economy to evolve the Soviet system cautiously.

28. B

A. The problem in the cartoon is not confusion but a lack of bread. A system that produced enough bread would not rely on long lines.

B. The Soviet system was inefficient in its creation of products and distribution. A more efficient system would not have long lines.

C. There is no indication that the people in the cartoon are involved in the creation of products.

D. Urban overpopulation exists in many cities and does not cause food line ups.

APPENDICES

TERMS AND PHRASES

The following are a list of terms and phrases that grade 9 Social Studies students should be familiar with.

USA

Abraham Darby
Adam Smith
Assembly Line Automation
Beliefs and values
Capital
Change
Charles Townshend
Corporations
Division of Labour
Eli Whitney
empire
flying shuttle
Free enterprise
Henry Ford
Immigration
Industrialization
Interchangeable parts
James Hargreaves
James Watt
Jethro Tull
John D. Rockefeller
Labour
laissez-faire
Land
Lifestyles resulting from a market economy
Market economy
Mass production
Mechanical Reaper
Mechanization
Mixed economy
Modernization
political stability
Pony express
power loom
Private enterprise
Productivity
raw materials
Richard Arkwright
Robert Blakewell
Samuel Colt
Samuel Slater
Scarcity
Specialization
spinning jenny
subsistence agriculture
Telegraph
Telephone
Textile industry
The Agricultural Revolution
The business cycle
The domestic system
The enclosure movement
The factory system
The Industrial Revolution
The role of consumers
The role of entrepeneurs
The role of government
The role of labour
The social, economic, spiritual, and physical impact of the market system
Thomas Edison
Transcontinental railroad
Transportation
Urbanization
water frame

USSR

Agrarian society
Area
Beliefs and values
Bolshevik Revolution
Centralization of authority
Climate
Collectives
Collectivism
Communism
Control economy
Czar Nicholas II
Economic conditions in Russia prior to 1917
Economic planning
Equality
Five Year Plans
Freedom of Choice
Glasnost
Gorbachev
GOSPLAN
incentive
individualism
Job security
Karl Marx
Lenin
Lifestyles resulting from a centrally planned system
Location
Market economy

materialism
Mixed economy
Natural Resources
Needs versus wants
Perestroika
Physical features
Population distribution
price controls
Russian society prior to 1917
Security
Serfdom
Socialism
Stalin
The 1917 Revolution
The New Economic Policy
The role of consumers
The role of government
The role of labour
The social, economic, spiritual, and physical impact of central planning
Trotsky
Vegetation

CANADA

Computers
How lifestyles in a mixed economy are different from those in a pure market or pure centrally planned economy
Innovation
Labour management relations
Lifestyles resulting from a mixed economy
Primary industry
Robotics
Secondary industry
Tertiary industry
The importance of the public sector
The information revolution
The social, economic, political, environmental, and cultural impact of technological change
The social, economic, spiritual, and physical impact of the mixed economy
Utilization of technology

MISCELLANEOUS

Command economy
Competition
Great Depression
means of production
Monopoly
supply and demand
trigger industry
Universal health care

CREDITS

1. Some cartoons are reprinted with the permission of Randy Glasbergen. WWW.GLASBERGEN.COM.
2. Some cartoons are reprinted with the permission of Carroll/Simpson.
3. Images are reproduced under a license agreement with www.clipart.com.

2000 Provincial Achievement Test

Questions 5 and 6 From *The Impact of the Industrial Revolution* by Nicholas B. Fessenden (Harcourt Brace Jovanovich, 1978).

Question 9 From *Spotlight Canada* by J. Bradley Cruxton and W. Douglas Wilson (Oxford University Press, 1988).

Questions 12 to 14 Table adapted from *Stalin's Russia 1924–41* by Bernard Barker (Basil Blackwell Publishers, 1979).

Questions 20 and 21 Source I. Cartoon by Jim Unger. Herman ® is reprinted with permission from LaughingStock Licensing Inc., Ottawa Canada. All rights reserved. Source II. BIZARRO © by Dan Piraro.

Question 24 From *Our Economy: How It Works* (Addison-Wesley Publishing Company, 1980).

Question 29 Cartoon by Edd Uluschak. Cartoon from *The Edmonton Journal*.

Questions 33 and 34 From *Industrialism: The American Experience* by James E. Bruner, Jr. (Glencoe Publishing Co., Inc., 1980).

Question 42 Cartoon by Gable from *The Globe and Mail*.

Questions 43 and 44 Source I. From *A New World Emerges* by David J. Rees (Arnold Publishing, 1994).

Question 45 Source I. Henry Thoreau. From *Environmental Concerns: The World* (Harcourt Brace Jovanovich, Inc., 1977). Public Domain.
Source II. Charles Lindberg. From *Environmental Concerns: The World* (Harcourt Brace Jovanovich, Inc., 1977). Public Domain.

Question 47 TOLES © The Buffalo News.

Questions 48 and 49 Phyllis A. Arnold. *The Soviet Union*. Edmonton: Arnold Publishing, 1983. Page 211.

Question 52 Cartoon by Malcolm Mayes from *Portfoolio 6* (Macmillan of Canada).

Questions 53 and 54 Maps adapted from *SCHOLASTIC WORLD CULTURES: THE SOVIET UNION AND EASTERN EUROPE*, Revised Edition by Hope T. Ludlow. Copyright © 1980, 1973 by Scholastic Inc.

2001 Provincial Achievement Test

Question 5 Illustrations I and II. Illustrations from *Witness History Series: The Industrial Revolution* by Nigel Smith [Wayland (Publishers) Limited, 1990].

Question 7 J. Bradley Cruxton and W. Douglas Wilson. From *Spotlight Canada*, New Edition (Oxford University Press, 1988).

Questions 10 and 11 Quotes by James Watson, Greg Bear, Jeremy Cherfas, and Paul Marango. From *Canada: Towards the 21st Century* by Helmut Manzl (Educational Media Press, 1991).

Questions 12 and 13 Cartoon I. Cartoon by Jim Unger. From *Canada in a Changing World: Geography*, Teacher's Guide, by Jack Cresswell (Harcourt Brace Jovanovich Canada Inc., 1989).
Cartoon II. BIZARRO © by Dan Piraro.

Question 14 Nicholas B. Fessenden. From *The Impact of the Industrial Revolution* (Harcourt Brace Jovanovich, Inc., 1978).

Question 18 Graphs from *World Powers in the Twentieth Century* by Harriet Ward (The British Broadcasting Corporation and Heinemann Educational Books Ltd., 1978).

Question 20 Quote by Stalin. From *Russia and the USSR: 1905–56* by John Laver (Hodder and Stoughton Educational, 1997). Public domain.

Question 24 Victor Kamber. From *USA Today*, July 1984 as found in *Economics in America: Opposing Viewpoints* by David L. Bender and Bruno Leone. (Greenhaven Press, Inc., 1986).

Question 28 Cartoon by Matt Wuerker. From *Looking Forward: Participatory Economics for the Twenty First Century* by Michael Albert and Robin Hahnel (South End Press, 1991).

Questions 35 and 36 James E. Bruner, Jr. From *Industrialism: The American Experience* (Glencoe Publishing Co., Inc., 1980).

Question 40 Charles R. Graham. From "So I told the Wright brothers It'll never work" as found in *Sunshine Sketches of a Little Economics* (Canadian Life Insurance Association).

Question 42 Bernard Harbor. From *The Breakup of the Soviet Union* [Wayland (Publishers) Ltd., 1992].

Questions 43 and 44 Phyllis A. Arnold. *The Soviet Union.* Edmonton: Arnold Publishing, 1983. Page 211.

Question 45 Cartoons I and II by Adrian Raeside. From *The Victoria Times-Colonist* as found in *The Demented Decade: The Mulroney Years—What Really Happened...* by Adrian Raeside (Doubleday Canada Limited, 1993).

Questions 48 and 49 Source I. Chart from *A New World Emerges* by David J. Rees (Arnold Publishing, 1994).

Questions 51 and 52 Maps adapted from *SCHOLASTIC WORLD CULTURES: THE SOVIET UNION AND EASTERN EUROPE*, Revised Edition by Hope T. Ludlow. Copyright © 1980, 1973 by Scholastic Inc.

Question 55 Cartoon by Bill Garner. From *The Washington Times* as found in *Best Editorial Cartoons of the Year, 1992 Edition* edited by Charles Brooks (Pelican Publishing Company, Inc., 1992).

NOTES

ORDERING INFORMATION

All School Orders

School Authorities are eligible to purchase these resources by applying the Learning Resource Credit Allocation (LRCA – 25% school discount) on their purchase through the Learning Resources Centre (LRC). Call LRC for details.

THE KEY Study Guides are specifically designed to assist students in preparing for unit tests, final exams, and provincial examinations.

KEY Study Guides – $29.95 each plus G.S.T.

SENIOR HIGH		JUNIOR HIGH	ELEMENTARY
Biology 30 Chemistry 30 English 30-1 English 30-2 Math 30 (Pure) Math 30 (Applied) Physics 30 Social Studies 30 Social Studies 33	Biology 20 Chemistry 20 English 20-1 Math 20 (Pure) Physics 20 Social Studies 20 English 10-1 Math 10 (Pure) Science 10 Social Studies 10	Language Arts 9 Math 9 Science 9 Social Studies 9 Math 8 Math 7	Language Arts 6 Math 6 Science 6 Social Studies 6 Math 4 Language Arts 3 Math 3

Student Notes and Problems (SNAP) Workbooks contain complete explanations of curriculum concepts, examples, and exercise questions.

SNAP Workbooks – $29.95 each plus G.S.T.

SENIOR HIGH		JUNIOR HIGH	ELEMENTARY
Chemistry 30 Math 30 Pure Math 30 Applied Math 31 Physics 30	Chemistry 20 Math 20 Pure Math 20 Applied Physics 20 Math 10 Pure Math 10 Applied Science 10	Math 9 Science 9 Math 8 Math 7	Math 6 Math 5 Math 4 Math 3

Visit our website for a "tour" of resource content and features at
<u>www.castlerockresearch.com</u>

Castle Rock Research Corp

#2340, 10180 – 101 Street
Edmonton, AB Canada T5J 3S4
e-mail: learn@castlerockresearch.com

Phone: 780.448.9619
Toll-free: 1.800.840.6224
Fax: 780.426.3917

SCHOOL ORDER FORM

THE KEY	QUANTITY
Biology 30	
Chemistry 30	
English 30-1	
English 30-2	
Math30 (Pure)	
Math 30 (Applied)	
Physics 30	
Social Studies 30	
Social Studies 33	
Biology 20	
Chemistry 20	
English 20-1	
Math 20 (Pure)	
Physics 20	
Social Studies 20	
English 10-1	
Math 10 (Pure)	
Science 10	
Social Studies 10	
Language Arts 9	
Math 9	
Science 9	
Social Studies 9	
Math 8	
Math 7	
Language Arts 6	
Math 6	
Science 6	
Social Studies 6	
Math 4	
Math 3	
Language Arts 3	

SNAP WORKBOOKS Notes and Problems/ Student Notes and Problems	QUANTITY Workbooks	QUANTITY Solutions Manuals
Chemistry 30		
Chemistry 20		
Physics 30		
Physics 20		
Math 30 Pure		
Math 30 Applied		
Math 31		
Math 20 Pure		
Math 20 Applied		
Math 10 Pure		
Math 10 Applied		
Science 10		
Science 9		
Math 9		
Math 8		
Math 7		
Math 6		
Math 5		
Math 4		
Math 3		

TOTALS

KEYS	
WORKBOOKS	
SOLUTION MANUALS	

Learning Resources Centre

Castle Rock Research is pleased to announce an exclusive distribution arrangement with the Learning Resources Centre (LRC). Under this agreement, schools can now place all their orders with LRC for order fulfillment. As well, these resources are eligible for applying the Learning Resource Credit Allocation (LRCA) which gives schools a 25% discount off LRC's selling price. Call LRC for details.

Orders may be placed with LRC by
telephone: (780) 427-5775,
fax: (780) 422-9750,
internet: www.lrc.learning.gov.ab.ca
or mail: 12360 - 142 Street NW
Edmonton, AB T5L 4X9.

PAYMENT AND SHIPPING INFORMATION

Name: ____________________

School Telephone: ____________________

SHIP TO
School: ____________________
Address: ____________________
City: ____________ Postal Code: ________

PAYMENT
☐ by credit card
VISA/MC Number: ____________ Expiry Date: ________
Name on Card: ____________________
☐ enclosed cheque
☐ invoice school P.O. number: ____________

Castle Rock Research Corp
#2340, 10180 – 101 Street, Edmonton, AB T5J 3S4 Tel: 780.448.9619 Fax: 780.426.3917
email: learn@castlerockresearch.com Toll-free: 1.800.840.6224
www.castlerockresearch.com